THE
PEP BOYS
AUTO GUIDE
TO CAR CARE
AND MAINTENANCE

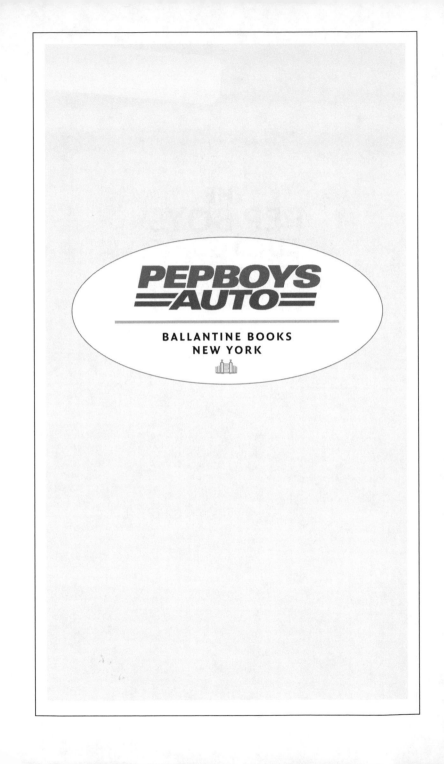

BALLANTINE BOOKS
NEW YORK

THE
PEP BOYS
AUTO GUIDE
TO CAR CARE
AND MAINTENANCE

E. J. Braswell

Note: This publication is intended to convey a basic understanding of the principles of car maintenance. It is sold with the understanding that the author, publisher, and The Pep Boys are not engaged in rendering professional services in our book. If the reader requires personal assistance or advice, a competent professional should be consulted.

The author, publisher, and The Pep Boys specifically disclaim any responsibility for any liability, loss, or risk, personal or otherwise, which is incurred as a consequence, directly or indirectly, of the use and application of any of the contents of this book.

A Ballantine Books Trade Paperback Original

Copyright © 2005 by The Pep Boys—Manny, Moe, and Jack

All rights reserved.

Published in the United States by Ballantine Books, an imprint of The Random House Publishing Group, a division of Random House, Inc., New York.

All photographs are courtesy of The Pep Boys.

Timeline created by Marian Calabro.

BALLANTINE and colophon are registered trademarks of Random House, Inc.

Library of Congress Cataloging-in-Publication Data is available from the publisher upon request.

ISBN 0-345-47685-9

Printed in the United States of America

Ballantine Books website address: www.ballantinebooks.com

2 4 6 8 9 7 5 3 1

Book design by Carole Lowenstein

ACKNOWLEDGMENTS

This book is for everyone at Dynasty: Peter, Chris, Pedro, Kim, Henry—and everyone else whose name I *should* know by now. I honestly could not have finished the book without you.

Thank you to Bruce Chidsey, who made sure all the information in the book was accurate and user friendly.

Special thanks to cousin Steve, Sheperd Todd, Maggie Libby, and my editor/driving companion, Jen Osborne.

CONTENTS

THE
PEP BOYS
AUTO GUIDE
TO CAR CARE
AND MAINTENANCE

A History of the Pep Boys

Manny, Moe, and Jack: Trust Is the Chassis

In 1921, four street-smart entrepreneurs from South Philadelphia each pitched in $200 to start an automotive accessories business.

Emmanuel "Manny" Rosenfeld, two Moes—Maurice "Moe" Strauss and Moe Radavitz—and W. Graham "Jack" Jackson were World War I navy buddies.

With their pooled $800 the partners rented a store at 7-11 North 63rd Street in West Philadelphia; there was just enough left over to cover an outlay of $63 to a car parts wholesaler and a few weeks of salaries for themselves. The address seemed lucky; it gave them the idea to include a pair of dice in their early signs and ads. As the four were setting up shop and suggesting names to go with it, Moe Strauss happened to glance at a carton of Pep Valve Grinding compound: Pep Auto Supply Company became the company's name for its first two years. "The Pep Boys" name arose courtesy of a policeman at 63rd and Market, who would advise motorists when he stopped them for equipment violations to "go see the boys at Pep" for a replacement oil wick (what passed for headlights in those days).

Moe Strauss was the guiding force. After leaving the navy he had tried to start his own auto accessories store twice. While both attempts failed, Moe stood firm in his belief that there was a need for such stores; car ownership throughout the country was skyrocketing. Finally, with help from the right partners—and a job as a cigar salesman to tide him over—he succeeded on his third attempt.

Manny was a great foil for Moe, with a head for figures and an easy-going personality that balanced Moe's quick temper. He also brought retail experience to the mix from a stint selling shoes at Lit Brothers, a leading Philadelphia department store at the time.

Moe Radavitz brought money and personal energy to the business, but left after a few years, leaving only one Moe; Moe Strauss.

There were actually two Jacks; unlike Manny Rosenfeld and Moe Strauss, neither one stayed with Pep Boys for long. The first was W. Graham Jackson, a navy buddy of Manny and Moe's and a cofounder of the business. Jack's boyish face appeared in very early logos. He must have been important to the business because he drew the biggest salary: $25 a week. After he left, one of Moe's brothers, Isadore ("Izzy"), took Jack's place—both in the company and as the caricature of Jack. Izzy even began signing his business letters I. M. "Jack" Strauss. In 1929, however, he struck out on his own. He moved to New York and founded Strauss Stores, which became R&S/Strauss and is now Strauss Discount Auto.

Sears, Roebuck & Co. had gotten into the auto accessories business early through its mail-order catalog, but Manny and Moe believed that people preferred to shop locally. Only in mortar-and-brick stores could customers touch the goods and ask for advice. An early slogan promised: "There's a Pep Store Near Your Door."

Pep Boys offered a further advantage: It was the first chain in the country to specialize in auto accessories rather than just offer them as a sideline. If they could keep prices low, customer service high, and the work ethic strong, there was no reason they shouldn't dominate the automotive aftermarket that they helped pioneer.

Stores stayed open six days a week, and the founders worked on Sundays as well: Local blue laws forbade them from actually opening the store. "Life for us at that time began around 6:15 A.M. and continued on until about 1:00 A.M, seven days each and every week," Manny remembers. "There was not much opportunity to reflect upon the past or dream of the future. Rather, we were more concerned about where the next meal was coming from."

All the hard work paid off a few years later when they opened their first branch—against the advice of their friends.

Pep Boys outfitted Rear Admiral Richard E. Byrd's second Antarctic expedition with two Kellett K2 Autogiros (a small, maneuverable craft with a plane fuselage and helicopter like rotors), a pilot, and a large supply of Pep Boys Snowman brand antifreeze. Pictured here after the September 22, 1933, presentation ceremony are Emmanuel "Manny" Rosenfeld (front row, second from left), Admiral Byrd (front row, third from left), and Maurice "Moe" Strauss (second row, left).

In 1923, with the business on solid footing, Manny and Moe were finally able to take a vacation/business research trip: a cross-country journey from Philadelphia to Los Angeles in a brand-new Model T. The desire for long-distance car travel was burning like a fever among Americans, spawning a new landscape of motels, campgrounds, roadside eateries, and billboards. One particular sign that caught their eye was for a dress shop called Minnie, Maude & Mabel's. They came back home with "Manny, Moe & Jack" and the idea of opening stores in southern California.

The use of the founders' names seemed to call for faces to match. Harry Moscovitz, a commercial artist—and Philadelphia native—

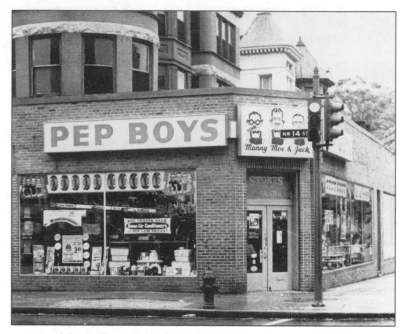

Founded and still proudly based in Philadelphia, Pennsylvania, Pep Boys was the neighborhood automotive parts and accessories store. As early advertisements used to proclaim, Manny, Moe, and Jack were "the three best friends your car ever had."

Manny, Moe, and Jack were used to full advantage in every advertising and media campaign the company produced, becoming popular American icons. Here they are shown with a variety of Pep Boys' private-label products like Cornell tires, Pure as Gold motor oil, and Cadet batteries.

These eight-foot-tall Manny, Moe & Jack statues adorned
many early Pep Boys and have become a much-sought-after item
for serious memorabilia collectors.

created the caricatures that are now icons of American marketing. The real Manny did wear glasses, sport a small mustache, and smoke a cigar. The real Moe was in fact taller, had a broad smile, and carefully waxed his winglike moustache every day.

Pep Boys continued to expand from Philadelphia and Los Angeles starting in 1933 with the opening of two stores, eventually developing the concept of the automotive Supercenter. Larger than early Pep Boys locations, these stores displayed more products and accessories than the competition, as well as maintaining attached automotive service centers.

Pep Boys now operates in thirty-six states and Puerto Rico, and is in the midst of a retail renewal, which began with the introduction of exciting new products and continues with dynamic store remodels throughout the chain. New store layouts feature the latest in interactive displays, brand-name products, and associates who are trained and ready to assist all Pep Boys customers.

Ready with a trusted, unbeatable sales and service team, Pep Boys truly offers "Parts, Service and So Much More."

CHAPTER 1

A Tutorial of Your Car and How It Works

Learning How to Drive

Sure, you know how to put the key in, shift into drive, and pull away—but do you really know exactly what goes on *inside* the car when you're out there on the road? You will by the end of this section! When you're done, you'll no longer think of your car as a Big Black Box, but as a logical sum of its fairly simple to understand parts.

Note: If you find this next part confusing or the terminology a little alien at first, don't worry. Continue to read through the next section on all the different systems in your car—and we'll go through all of this again. It *will* make sense—we promise.

When you put your key into the ignition and turn it, you close a switch that allows electricity to flow from the battery to the starter, an electric motor that starts turning the crankshaft. As the engine spins, the pistons and the fuel start pumping and the valves start opening and closing. Compression is achieved, the spark plugs fire, and the engine itself takes over. The starter then disengages itself from the process.

The fuel pump delivers gas to the cylinders of the engine through intake valves, where it is mixed with air and compressed by the pistons. This highly combustible mixture is lit by the spark plugs and explodes, forcing the pistons down, which then turns the crankshaft.

The crankshaft connects to the transmission, which determines with how much power and at what speed the wheels should turn. To shift gears, the car must first release the transmission from the crankshaft, and this is done by a clutch if it's a car with a manual shift. Power is converted hydraulically through a torque converter in an automatic, transferring engine power by the use of fluid.

In rear-wheel-drive vehicles, the driveshaft continues from the transmission on to the rear of the car, with a hinge on each end called a universal joint (or a CV joint in a front-wheel-drive car) to keep the whole thing flexible and from snapping like a twig when the car hits a bump. A differential (sometimes called a rear end) at the end of the driveshaft delivers the turning power of the shaft and converts the power through a ring and pinion gears "sideways" to the two rear wheels and determines the difference in speed that each wheel must have in order for you to execute a turn. When turning, the outside wheel must turn faster than the inside wheel or you would break the axles or gears. The differential is what allows this to happen.

In front-wheel-drive cars there is a transaxle instead of a transmission, which handles gear-shifting as well as the individual speed of the left and right front tires for when you want to turn.

Oil keeps everything lubricated and operating quietly and properly.

. . . Now, that wasn't so hard, was it?

Okay, it was. So now let's break down your car system by system and go through each one simply and clearly. We'll put it all together at the end of this section again—and you'll be amazed by how much you've already learned.

Breakdown: Your Car, System by System

ENGINE

Okay. This is actually a far simpler thing than you might imagine. Relax, take a deep breath and imagine yourself in a tropical paradise . . . on a bicycle.

In the same way that bicycle pedals go up and down, the crankshaft in a car pumps up and down, transferring rotation and power to the wheels.

But instead of legs (and feet), a car engine has pistons that push down on the crankshaft. The pistons are propelled downward by an explosion above them in the cylinder. So the more cylinders you have, the more pistons you have; the more feet pedaling on the bike, the faster and more powerful the bike—er, the car. This is why a V8 is so much more powerful than a V6 or a four-cylinder engine.

(The V refers to how the cylinders are set up. Either they're in line and called an inline 4, 6, or 8, or sort of alternately positioned like the two tops of a V. They can also be directly opposing each other in a flat design, as in old VWs.)

How the explosion occurs is where our little human-and-bicycle metaphor breaks down. It takes four cycles or up-and-downs to make things happen.

1. As the pistons move down, a mixture of gas and air is sucked into the cylinder through the intake valve.
2. As the piston heads back up, it creates compression, and the gas mixture is lit (or detonated, if you want to be precise) by a spark plug, which—you guessed it—creates a little spark. It's kind of like the electric ignition on a gas stove that causes the burner to light.
3. The resulting explosion (in the cylinder, not your stove) pushes the piston back down against the crankshaft with power, the transmission transmits this power to the wheels, and your car goes zooming off.
4. As the piston comes back up the exhaust valve lets out the burned gases, and the cycle starts all over again.

Back to your bike. Even if it's instinctive by now, your brain figures out which leg pushes down to keep your bike rolling smoothly. If you tried to push down both legs at once, nothing would happen. The same thing is true with a car—the pistons have to push down on the crankshaft in precisely timed movements. Ignition, or spark, is timed exactly when the piston nears the top so the explosion will force the piston back down again.

ELECTRICAL

The electrical system in your car does three important things:

1. It cranks your engine to help it start.
2. It makes your car start once it's cranking by causing the spark plugs to fire.
3. It runs all the electric devices in your car; the headlights, the radio, the fan, the computers . . .

Starting Your Car

When you put your key into the ignition and turn it, you're doing two things. First, you're closing a circuit that allows a current to run from the battery to the starter motor. Second, the starter gear physically moves into and engages the flywheel. The starter is a little electric motor that jump-starts your car by turning a flywheel that then turns the crankshaft, causing the pistons to go up and down, beginning their cycle. When your car has started—and you let your key turn back—the motor disengages itself from the engine, which is now merrily chugging along of its own accord.

Running Your Car

At the same time you start your car and electricity flows to the starter motor, some electricity also goes to a coil that amplifies the voltage to about 50,000 volts. (And yes, that's more than enough to kill you, especially if you have heart problems, so be very careful.) From there the current runs to your engine through the distributor cap in an older car or the coil wire on a newer one, sending that 50,000-volt spark of electricity to each of your (yes, you guessed it) spark plugs. The voltage or pressure of the current is so great at this point that it leaps across the open space between the two electrodes of the spark plug in the cylinder. The spark sets off an explosion of gas and air in the cylinder, and the piston fires, the cycle begins, and off you go.

Running Other Things

Everything in your car that draws electrical juice—the fan in the heater, the map light, the computer that controls your engine, your

CD player, etc.—is capable of having its expensive inner parts fried if there's a sudden overload of electricity, which happens more often than you might think. That's why the current for each one runs through a fuse. Think of a fuse as a really weak, badly made lightbulb: The slightest power surge causes the filament inside to burn out. In the same way, a fuse blows out if there's a problem in the system to stop the electricity from traveling any farther up the line and damaging anything.

The fuse box for most of the passenger and driver utilities (radio, map light, etc.) is somewhere under or behind the dashboard; for the onboard computer, fuel pumps, and other operational items, the fuse box is often under the hood in the engine compartment.

If a fuse blows, it generally means you have a problem with a component in that system or that a wire has rubbed up against a metal part and is grounded out. Merely replacing the fuse generally will not fix the problem. *Never* replace the fuse with one with a higher value.

Your Battery and Alternator

The electricity to start your car is stored in the battery, just as the electricity to power a flashlight is stored in its batteries. Unlike a flashlight, however, your car battery is recharged every time you run the car from the power of the engine. An alternator (really a generator) runs off a drive belt attached to the engine, and converts this physical power into electricity, sending it to the battery and all of the other components in the car that require electrical power.

Efficient, no?

On most cars the red-colored terminal on a battery is positive and the black is negative. Whenever doing *any* work on the battery, always remember to disconnect the black or negative side first—this prevents everything in your car from getting fried if there's a problem.

As batteries age and distribute and receive recharges, they get white hair just as we do, in the form of a powder that will appear on the top. Once the battery is disconnected properly this can be cleaned up harmlessly, but eventually, like all batteries, it will have to be replaced when it fails to perform.

OIL

You probably know a lot about this system already. Oil helps lubricate and clean all the different metal parts that would otherwise grind against one another in the engine, destroying your car. It's stored in the oil pan when the car is turned off; when the car is running, it's pumped around the moving parts of the engine by an oil pump, lubricating as it goes. An oil filter cleans out the sludge and particles. A dipstick lets you check how much oil you have (as well as its quality), and an oil filler nearby lets you add more when it's low—or refill completely when you're changing the oil.

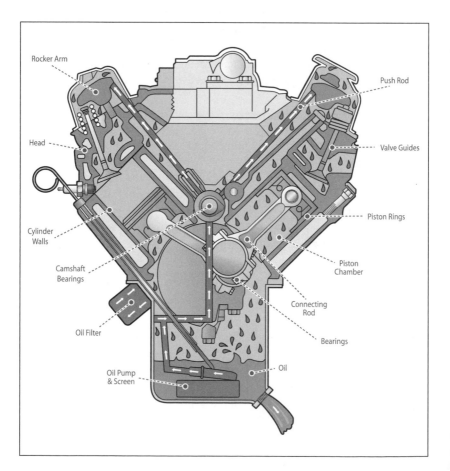

Reading a Can or Bottle of Oil

We'll say this again later when we talk about checking, filling, and changing your oil, but we'll say it now just to make sure it's burned into your head: *Only buy the kind of oil recommended in your vehicle's owner's manual.*

Like any other liquid, oil is thinner when hot and thicker when cold (on its way to freezing). This texture or ease of flow is known as viscosity; high viscosity means thick and sludgy, and low means thin and watery. Oil needs to remain thin enough when cold to flow and lubricate everything completely when starting and thick enough to "stick" to the parts it's lubricating when hot.

Most oil you buy is multiviscosity, so that you don't have to switch types at different times of the year. The numbers on a can that say something like 20W-50 indicate the range; the higher the number (50) the higher the viscosity, the lower the number (20), the lower the viscosity. The letter W after a number, usually on the lower end of the range, indicates that the oil has been winter tested.

The quality of oil for a gas-powered car begins with an S and is followed by a letter, with A being the lowest. If you have a new car, your manual will probably recommend SL or SJ. Higher quality oils can always be used for cars whose manuals suggest lower quality oils; the reverse, however, is not true. In fact, SA through SH are considered obsolete now—it's best just to never use them.

Oil is not the place to begin penny-pinching with your car; always make sure it's a quality brand that has been certified by the American Petroleum Institute and says "Energy Conserving."

(If you drive under tough conditions—towing a trailer, navigating hilly areas, or just high-speed driving—you may want to consider the added performance of synthetic oil. Synthetics cost more but can help extend the life of your engine.)

HEATING/COOLING

For Your Car

If you hadn't already figured it out by now, with all those explosions going on in your engine, the bigger issue is *cooling* rather than heating.

Temperatures can reach over a thousand degrees under the hood, and if left unchecked things could start to melt. To keep this from happening, your car's engine is equipped with a liquid cooling system (unless it's equipped with an air-cooled engine).

Coolant is stored primarily in the radiator. When the engine is running, a pump runs the coolant into a hose at the bottom of the radiator and through the water jacket around the engine, where the liquid picks up heat. Coolant is then carried back to the radiator via a hose in its top. The radiator in your car works similarly to one you might find in a house: It helps *radiate* the heat off and out of the coolant and into the air (in front of the grille), with the help of a fan when the car isn't moving to flow air across the fins of the radiator to remove the heat. The now cooled-down coolant gets pumped back into the engine, and the process starts all over again.

There will often be a coolant reservoir next to the radiator; if there is, you add coolant there instead of directly into the radiator. When coolant heats up it expands (as do most liquids), and the reservoir catches the extra when it overflows the system to keep it from leaking all over the ground. Leaked coolant is actually more of a hazard than a lot of the other toxic chemicals that could leak out of your car.

Coolant is usually a mixture of water and antifreeze; this fluid has a higher boiling point than water and a lower freezing point. The antifreeze is usually ethylene glycol. Ethylene glycol tastes sweet and is *deadly poisonous*. Dogs love it. Small children love it. Even a tablespoonful can be fatal. So be very careful where you keep extra and when you refill the reservoir or radiator—clean any spills *immediately*.

For You

Heating is easy! Heat from the engine is carried via the heated coolant to a small radiator behind the dashboard, and just like the engine radiator this one dissipates heat and a fan distributes it through the appropriate vents.

Air-Conditioning

Cooling is . . . not so easy. Basically, a liquid called a refrigerant is pushed through an evaporator, where it absorbs and removes heat from inside the car. It does this because it has a very low boiling point (mean-

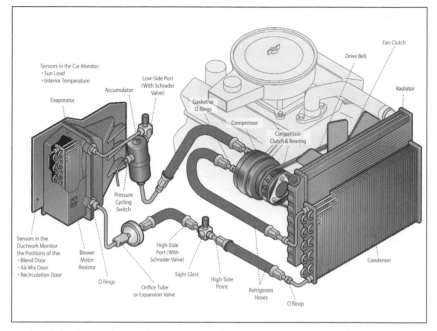

ing it boils at a lower temperature than plain water), and when a liquid turns into a gas it picks up heat. From there it gets sucked into a compressor—taking the heat with it—where it's compressed, then fed down a radiator-like device called a condenser. This is generally located in front of your engine coolant radiator. There the gas condenses, turning back into a liquid (think of the water droplets that form on the inside of a glass kettle after the water stops boiling and cools down), releasing the heat through the car's radiator. From there this high-pressure liquid is fed through a small orifice called an expansion valve (or orifice tube) and converted back to a low-pressure liquid, then sent onward to the evaporator again.

This process is complicated—you'll notice we didn't bother to include any of the words in the glossary—and the whole system is best left to a technician if anything goes wrong.

FUEL

Diesel! Ethanol! Methanol! Fuel cells! Leaded! Unleaded! *Aaaaaaah!*

Relax. We're going to deal with "normal" unleaded gas, the kind you usually get at the pump. There are only three things you really need to know about it.

First of all, gas isn't just gas; it's usually gas plus detergents, which help keep your engine clean.

Second, gas "quality" is measured in octane. The octane rating indicates how likely the gas is to explode badly in the cylinders, misfiring and causing what is technically known as a spark "knock" or a "ping." Gas with a higher octane burns completely and more smoothly; gas with a lower octane burns faster (and less smoothly). Check your owner's manual for the octane that's best suited to your engine; use anything lower and you could be damaging the engine, and use anything higher and you're probably wasting money on something you don't need.

And third, your car *doesn't* run on gas. It runs on a mixture of gas and oxygen; in fact, most of the explosion that moves the pistons is air!

And here is how it all works.

The fuel pump in your car—either mechanical (driven by the engine) or electrical (powered by the battery and alternator)—brings the

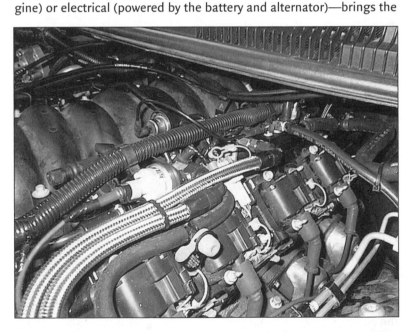

gas from the tank to the engine through the fuel filter. Air comes into the engine via an air inlet hose or snorkel or through a filter.

In the days of carburetors, the throttle plate hooked to your gas pedal would determine the amount of air and fuel going into the engine, and the throttle would determine the ratio of gas to air when you pressed down on the accelerator. Today all cars have electronic fuel systems with computers and injectors, which decide how potent a cocktail of gas and air gets injected into the cylinders. In this case, consider air the alcohol and gas the mixer; the more *air*, the bigger the kick!

You should always keep your tank at least a quarter full; even with a filter, crud and grit collects at the bottom of the tank—and you *really* don't want that going through your engine. Also, keep track of your mileage and compare it to what the manual says your car should get; if you're consistently less than normal that means there could be a problem.

TRANSMISSION/DRIVETRAIN

Think about this statement carefully: Engine rotation does *not* equal wheel rotation (except in highest gear in some cars). If it did, your car would have all the power of a unicycle, which goes exactly as fast as the pedals are pumped. And you might have noticed there are no unicycles in the Tour de France!

As with many things in life, you can only have one of two things at any given time in a car: power (torque) *or* speed.

Welcome back to our bike metaphor! In almost exactly the same way you shift gears on your bike to generate more power or speed, your car needs to shift gears to do the same thing.

Imagine the gears on the bike moving. You can see that for every single rotation of the big gear, the smaller turns many more times—and at a faster rate than the big gear does. The same is true for a car; in high gear the wheels turn several times for every single rotation of the larger "engine" gear—which means they turn a lot faster. Because you have speed, you don't have power, which is why you're in high gear during highway driving but not when you're going uphill, starting up, or pulling a heavy load.

In low gear, the wheel gear only turns once for every several turns of the engine gear (about 2.5 to 1); the engine gear turns faster and the wheel gear *slower*. That means more power to the wheels. This is why you use it to go up steep hills or to start the car moving, but not to travel at high speed.

(Actually, in cars at low gear the wheel and engine gears are approximately the *same* size, so the car goes slowly with the full power of the engine.)

The "gear box" in a car is called a transmission.

Because there's no "chain" in a car and the crankshaft is connected more or less directly to the transmission, the engine has to disengage itself physically from the gears so the engine does not stall when stopped. You do this with the clutch in a manual transmission; the car does it for you in an automatic transmission, using a torque converter.

Out the other side of the transmission, the crankshaft is now called a driveshaft. It leads to the differential in a rear-wheel-drive car, which turns the rotation of the shaft ninety degrees to move the wheels forward. The differential also determines the individual speed of each wheel when you turn: The inside wheel turns slower, the outer wheel faster.

In front-wheel-drive vehicles, the differential and the transmission are combined into the transaxle.

STEERING/SUSPENSION

Repairs and service to the system are generally known as *front end work*, since the rear wheels don't do any steering on most cars. Your steering wheel is connected to a steering column that probably controls a rack-and-pinion steering system. The wheels are connected to the car at the steering linkage by means of ball joints, which allow a freedom of movement to the wheels, just as your upper arm does in your shoulder socket.

The suspension system keeps your car from flying up into the air every time you hit a bump. Springs suspend the vehicle and let the wheels maintain contact with the ground at (almost) all times, expanding if there's a pothole and compressing if there's a bump. But springs don't just expand and contract in one smooth motion—picture taking a big jump on an old spring bed. It keeps bouncing for a while long after you stop; in a car, this would keep you happily carsick for the entire length of the journey. Shock absorbers smooth out and slow down the rest of the bounces, just as the cylinder on a storm door keeps it from slamming shut.

There are two basic kinds of suspension. The double wishbone has a pair of control arms that cradle the wheel at their wide end and the spring and shock absorber at the narrow end where they come together.

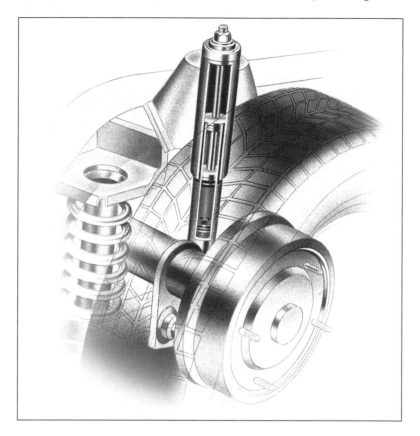

A MacPherson strut is more like a vertical rod and acts as both the spring part of the suspension and as a shock absorber.

BRAKES

There are two different kinds of brakes—drum and disc—but both operate on the same two basic principles; friction, and the fact that liquids don't compress. Think of a sealed juice box: When you squeeze it, does the box get smaller as it forces the liquid into itself, or does it explode juice out the top and all over you?

Putting your foot down on the brake forces brake fluid out of a hydraulic master cylinder. The fluid then goes into the brake lines and up to the brake cylinders that operate the brakes.

With disc brakes we can go right back to our bike metaphor. Just like the pair of calipers that squeeze against your bike tire to make it stop, there is a pair of calipers that squeeze the brake pads or friction material against the rotor, or disc, which is directly connected to the wheel. When you press the brake pedal, brake fluid is forced into pistons in the calipers. Because the fluid doesn't compress, it has no place to go, so it pushes harder and further against the pistons. This forces them out to make the pad press against the rotor. Friction causes the rotor, and therefore the wheel, to stop.

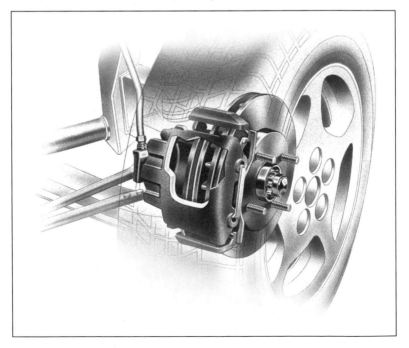

With drum brakes, instead of a disc directly connected to the wheel, there is a metal—you guessed it—drum. Inside the drum are a pair of brake shoes with a *wheel cylinder* between the two shoes, containing pistons, which are forced outward in the cylinder when brake fluid is forced into it (remember the whole liquids-not-compressing thing?). The pistons push out against the shoes (which are lined with the same material as disc brake pads), which in turn push against the inside of the wheel drum. Again, the friction created causes the drum, and therefore the wheel, to stop turning.

Power Braking

Today many cars have power braking; a power brake booster helps to force the brake fluid into the cylinders and calipers without much effort on your part.

Antilock/ABS Brakes

If you've slammed on your brakes in a car not equipped with ABS you've probably seen first-hand how an object in motion tends to stay in motion—and in the case of something as big and unwieldy as a car, not necessarily in the direction you want. This is why your parents always told you to pump the brake—slowing the car down in stages while you steer around whatever hazard you encountered. Antilock brakes do this for you with a computer and sensors that monitor wheel speed much faster than you could. Think of it as many tiny, measured brake pulses so you can keep moving forward (slowly) and steer around potential hazards, as opposed to slamming on traditional brakes and getting thrown all over the road.

THE EXHAUST SYSTEM

Noxious gases. Yes, they're the end product of the internal combustion engine—though many alternative fuels and engine types are being invented every day to help cut down on air pollution and gas usage.

After the explosions occur in the cylinders, the waste fumes exit through the engine's exhaust manifold—but not before the positive crankcase ventilation (PCV) valve catches some of the gases that escaped the cylinders into the crankcase, and sends them back into the engine so they can be utilized and reburned. The exhaust then travels down pipes to the catalytic converter, which uses oxygen, heat, and precious metals to convert most of the pollutants into water and carbon dioxide (CO_2). The gases that remain chug through the muffler to eliminate most of the noise and then go out into the environment through the tailpipe. An oxygen sensor monitors the fumes and sends the information back to the engine's computer, letting it know how to mix or rebalance the air/fuel ratio.

The emissions control system is only *part* of this system.

Maximum tire inflation recommendation
Never pump the tires higher than the recommended pounds per square inch rating (PSI). It can cause your car to lose traction when braking and will wear out your tires sooner.

Tire size code
These numbers show the tire's width in millimeters, aspect ratio (tire height divided by tire width), and wheel size. The letters refer to a number of things, such as whether the tire is a radial and what its maximum speed rating is:

S = 112 mph
H = 130 mph
V = over 130 mph

Load range rating
Tells how much weight each tire can support, which is important if you're towing a trailer or carrying very heavy loads.

TIRES

Yes, they count as a "system" too! In some ways, tires are the part of the car you should be most concerned with, since they are directly responsible for your safety. They deserve more than a half-hearted kick now and then to see if they're inflated properly; at the very least you should understand how to read the information on them and the simple tasks you can perform to keep them at their best.

How to read your tires

Materials description
Tells whether the tire is "tubeless" or "tube-type." Today almost all cars and light trucks use tubeless tires.

Uniform Tire Quality Grading (UTQG)
Gives ratings for tread wear, traction, and temperature.

Learning How to Drive, Take Two

Are you ready to start your engine again?

When you put your key into the ignition and turn it, you close a switch that allows electricity to flow from the battery to the starter, an electric motor that starts turning the crankshaft. This allows the pistons and the fuel to start pumping and the engine itself to take over. The starter then disengages itself from the process.

Electricity is also sent to your lights when you turn them on, as well as your radio and anything else that requires juice—and more of it is created from engine power by the alternator, which is then stored in the battery for future use.

The fuel pump delivers gas to the cylinders in the engine, where it is mixed with air and compressed by the pistons. An electric spark in the spark plugs lights this highly combustible mixture, which then explodes, forcing the pistons down, which turns the crankshaft. A computer controls the power and timing of the spark so the engine runs at maximum efficiency.

While this is going on the engine is getting hot enough to melt the metal around it. The coolant is pumped through its water jacket, picking up heat, and then takes it out to the radiator, where it cools off. If you're cold and turn on the heat in the car, some of this excess warmth gets fanned back into the passenger compartment.

The now-turning crankshaft leads into the transmission, which determines with how much power or at what speed the wheels should turn. To start driving you need to be in low gear, because the car needs a lot more power to start than once it is running on the highway. To shift gears the car must first release the transmission from the crankshaft; this is done by a clutch—or a torque converter in an automatic.

In front-wheel drive, you have a transaxle instead of a transmission, which handles gear-shifting as well as the individual speed of the left and right front tires for when you want to turn.

In rear-wheel drive, the driveshaft continues from the transmission to the back of the car, with a hinge at each end called a universal joint to keep the whole thing flexible and from snapping like a twig if the car hits a bump.

When you turn the steering column leads to a rack-and-pinion system, which guides the wheels left or right. At the same time, a differential at the end of the driveshaft in a rear-wheel-drive car delivers the turning power of the shaft "sideways" to the two wheels and determines the difference in speed that each wheel must have in order for you to execute that turn.

Going over that rock in your driveway doesn't send you into the bushes, because the springs in the suspension keep all four tires connected to the road, and you stay in your seat because shock absorbers cushion the resulting bounce.

On the highway you shift into high gear—or your car does it for you, in an automatic—which means less power but more speed. When it's time for you to stop, pushing on the brake pedal releases brake fluid, which causes the brake shoes and/or brake pads to squeeze up against the wheel, causing friction and a slow down.

Oil keeps everything from grinding against everything else and coming to a stop.

See? I'll bet you didn't even realize all the stuff you were learning. While it may not be *easy*, everything in a car makes logical, mechanical sense. And even if you just understand the basics it gives you a better idea how the whole thing works.

CHAPTER 2

Basic Car Care Maintenance That You Can Do Yourself

Top Ten Things You Need to Know About Your Car

Or, how not to look like a complete idiot at a garage.

If you ignore *everything else* in this chapter or book, make sure you at least know or can do everything in this list. It will save you a lot of grief, embarrassment, and scrambling around for information later.

1. **How to pump gas.** No joke—in some states, such as New Jersey and Oregon, it's full service only at all gas stations! So even if you've grown up there, you should go over state lines and learn how to "self-serve." You'll probably have to pump your own gas eventually, and it's a lot cheaper than sticking to full service all the time.

2. **How to open your hood.** Or how to release your parking or emergency brake. You'd be surprised how many people mistake the two.

3. **The make, model, and year of your car.** It's the first thing a technician will ask you every time.

4. **How many cylinders it has.** While this will come up less often, some models of cars are so similar that the only difference is whether it has a four-, six-, or eight-cylinder engine—which is important when you're looking for replacement parts.

5. **Where you keep your registration, insurance card, and owner's manual in the car.** "Excuse me, Officer; I know it's around here somewhere. . . ."

6. **How to use a jack and change a tire—*before* an emergency.** Even if *you* never have to, you might have to instruct someone else. And being on the side of the road with a flat is not the time to begin figuring out how to use the jack that came with your car.

7. **How to check and fill your oil, windshield wiper fluid, and coolant.** These are easy things you can do to maintain and extend the life of your car.

8. **Whether or not you have anti-lock brakes.** This determines how you *should* brake; whether you should pump them or just brake, let the ABS kick in, and continue to drive.

9. **What to do after you've been in an accident.** Even if you and your car come out of it okay, there are still things you must do for both legal as well as insurance reasons.

10. **Where the fuse box is.** Would you rather shell out for a new radio and the labor, or replace a fuse yourself?

Following Your Owner's Manual

Before we go any further, take your manual out of the car and look at it.
    We mean it.

You probably think of the manual as a thick, scary thing that sits in your glove compartment or trunk or on the floor, collecting dust. It seems completely unreadable, like the one that came with your computer.

In fact, car manufacturers have gone a long way in the last few years to make them easy to read, clear, nicely organized, and understandable by those of us without a career in the grease pit. It's really not so scary! Trust us!

A VIEW FROM THE TOP DOWN

For one thing, the manual probably has a top-down diagram of what's under the hood with everything labeled: coolant reservoir, battery, oil dipstick, oil filler, etc. One of the best—and easiest—things you can do is to take a spare fifteen minutes with your car and that page, finding each of the engine components for yourself.

IMPORTANT INFO

Remember Top 10 number 3? Not only will your manual tell you the make, model, and year of your car, but it also has a lot of other extremely important information—without which you risk not only shortening the life of your car, but severely damaging it as well. You might consider going through the manual and taking notes, keeping a list of the most important pieces of info at the front of the book for quick reference.

Maintenance Schedule

This is very, very important. In the back of your manual should be a schedule for everything from when and how often to change your oil to when you should have a complete tune-up. These things can vary from every 3,000 miles to every 60,000. Even if you choose to do none of this work yourself, following this schedule strictly will guarantee as long and healthy a life as possible for your car. Ignore what friends and relatives tell you about oil changes or checking the belts—just follow the schedule.

- **What octane of gas the car needs.** If you put in too low an octane, the engine won't work right, and at best your car will run with much less efficiency—at worst, you could damage your engine. If you put in too high an octane, you're wasting your money on something you don't need.

- **The capacity of the gas tank.** This will help you keep track of mileage and costs.

- **The extent of your warranty.** Again, don't pay for something you don't have to if something needs to be fixed that's covered by the warranty.

- **How the company that made your car defines severe driving.** Obviously you know that severe driving means more frequent oil changes, tune-ups, checkups, and the like—but did you know that "severe driving" can mean stop-and-go city traffic as well? Or driving on perfectly fine winter roads that have been salted?

- **Type of fluids you should buy and use.** Oil viscosity and rating, percentage of antifreeze to water in the coolant, what kind of automatic transmission fluid . . . Putting in the wrong fluids can damage your car. Always check your manual before adding or changing anything in your engine.

- **Where important but not easily visible car components are.** Such as your fuse box, oil filter, and even the location of the jack—which isn't always with the spare tire.

- **How-To.** While we give you the basics here on how to do a lot of your own basic maintenance, every car is a little different and their components may be in different places. Also, manuals will often take you through things such as changing your oil step-by-step, including diagrams and information specific to your car. Like what kind of oil to use, where to find the pan and filter, how much oil you need, and the replacement part number for the filter.

We're not asking you to read your manual from cover to cover (though it would be helpful if you did), but please, *please* take a look at it. You'll be glad you did.

Parts and Tools

Okay, now you've read your manual—or at least taken a look at it—and are ready for some real hands-on car work. While most of it won't require any special tools, here are a few things that will make your life easier:

- **Work gloves.** No, this isn't to protect dainty manicures. A lot of the stuff in, around, and on cars is unhealthy at best, and toxic at worst. Wear them. If you don't like the way they feel, get disposable latex gloves.

- **Safety glasses.** Do you *like* getting hot oil in your eyes?

- **Clean rags.** Things are going to get very dirty, and some things, like the oil drain plug, need to be wiped very clean.

- **Funnel.** Did we mention the toxicity and expense of the chemicals you put in your car?

- **Jack.** You probably already have this.

- **Jack stands.** Absolutely necessary if the car is on a jack. Under no circumstances should you perform any work underneath your car unless it is first supported by jack stands.

- **Socket wrench set.** If you're not particularly strong in the arms, consider getting a breaker bar extender so you can get more force for your push.

- **Lug wrench.** Again, you probably have this already with your jack; sometimes jacks have them sort of "built-in."

- **Filter wrench.** If possible, when looking for one try to bring an oil filter with you so you can buy the right size.

- **Screwdriver.** Both flathead and Phillips.

- **Wood blocks or wheel chocks.** To put up against the wheels when you're working on the car.

- **Tire pressure gauge.** Keep this easily accessible somewhere in the car so you can check the pressure when you have a minute or two of downtime—like at the gas station. If you can spare the cash, get one with a dial instead of the typical "stick" ones; they're easier to read and far more accurate.

- **Flashlight.** One of the newer ones with LEDs that allow you to focus the beam tightly would be really useful when you're trying to follow the path of a hose or belt, or look at something deep in the engine.

Be Careful!

Read this carefully before tinkering with your car!

1. *Never, ever* go underneath a car unless it's in park and has blocks placed firmly on both sides of at least two wheels.
2. *Never* go underneath a car that is only being held up by a tire jack. Always use jack stands, and carefully read the instructions that come with them.
3. For almost all maintenance that involves touching, opening, or filling things, the car must be completely cool so you don't burn yourself. Wait a minimum of forty-five minutes after you've turned it off.
4. There are many, *many* things on a car that can tear, scrape, burn, poison, bruise, itch, cut, lacerate, gash, damage, injure, rend, combust, mutilate, scald, mangle, wound, singe, and generally irk you. Always wear protective clothes and safety goggles, be careful, and use your head.

Do-It-Yourself Light Maintenance

It may sound a little compulsive, but consider keeping a notebook in your car or notes in the back of your manual of what you did and when. Do this not just for monthly checks and inspections, but for things such as changing the oil, changing the air filter, aiming the headlights, etc. Not only will this keep you organized, it may also help you save money by not forcing you to take your car in for the little things. For that matter, you should also keep the receipts and service forms from your garage so you can keep track of what *they* have done as well.

FAST, EASY, AND OFTEN
"At the Gas Tank"

Many people recommend doing some maintenance work every time you fill up. In reality, we realize this isn't too likely unless you're already a gearhead. Instead, try to perform the following checks and adjustments once a week or every couple of weeks. Once you get into the routine it will all go really quickly.

You'll notice we don't go into a lot of detail on exactly where you'll find things like the coolant reservoir or the battery. Remember earlier when we told you to go under the hood with your owner's manual and identify each of the major components of your engine?

- **Visual check.** In some ways, this is the most important "maintenance" work you can do. While it doesn't involve adding, changing, or adjusting anything, it will give you early warning if something is wrong with your car.

   The first few times you give your car the once-over (and even if you did your homework we still recommend doing it with the owner's manual in hand), it might seem a little intimidating. After a while, though, when you get to know how your car normally looks, you'll immediately be able to spot something that looks different. Oh, and by the way, we mean a visual check *under the hood* as well as just around your car.

   Some things to watch out for immediately are:
   - **Leaks.** Is there something pooling under the car when it's parked that's not the clear water of air conditioner condensate? Refer to our "fluid identifier" on page 86 to help diagnose the problem.
   - **Tire damage.** Bulges, punctures, slashes, unusual wear—anything that shouldn't be there.
   - **The battery terminals.** Are they clean? Covered in gunk? Dusted with a strange white powder that looks suspiciously like mold? While you don't have to do anything *immediately* at

the gas station, make a mental note to clean them when you get a few minutes. If the battery develops the white powder often, it could be a sign that your battery's getting old.

- **Tire inflation and pressure.** Incorrect tire pressure can reduce your mileage, decrease the car's handling, and increase the danger of a blowout. Low inflation is the number one cause of tire failure. On the other hand, do not inflate to the maximum inflation numbers on the tires—check the manual or door post, and do it early and often. Remember: A tire can lose up to half its air and still not look as if it's flat. And just when you think you're done . . . check your spare!

- **Checking inflation.** Always do it *before* driving, when your tires are cold: Driving heats up the tires and increases the pressure and inflation. The recommended maximum PSI is based on a cold tire.
  1. Unscrew the cap covering the valve stem.
  2. Place the gauge over the valve.
  3. Push down quickly and firmly so you don't lose any air.
  4. Hold it down until the gauge stops moving.
  5. Pull the gauge off the valve quickly and read the inflation.

- **Pumping your tires.** This is one of the easiest maintenance chores you can do, with the biggest impact on your car's health. Most gas stations have pumps, either free or coin operated, and some even allow you to select the right inflation manually before you start.

  And speaking of before-you-start, make sure the hose actually works and that there's air coming out of it—you can *deflate* a tire by using a pump that's not working right. Sometimes you can tell if air is coming out by pressing the inflation button on the hose's handle. If it doesn't have a button, you'll have to listen carefully for the sound of air rushing *into* the tire as soon as you start pumping. If you don't hear anything, stop pumping after a few seconds and check the pressure with a gauge to see if anything's happening.
  1. Place the hose valve over the tire's valve stem.
  2. Push the hose valve down on the tire. If there's an inflator button, hold it down as you hold the hose in place.
  3. Add only a little air at a time; it's easy to overinflate or even burst a tire by putting in too much air. Check the inflation as you go with a gauge if the hose doesn't have one built in.
  4. When you have the correct inflation, remove the hose and replace the cap on the valve stem.

- **Taking air out of your tires.** It can happen, especially if you don't pay attention when you're inflating them.
  1. Remove the valve cap and press the tip of a key into the valve to depress the pin there. Air will rush out.
  2. Do this for only a few seconds at a time, checking the air pressure as you go.
  3. When you have the right inflation, be sure to replace the valve cap.

Windshield Wiper Fluid

If checking the level of wiper fluid often seems a little silly to you, just remember the last time you drove with dust covering your windshield and the sun in your eyes, everything glowing and blurry. Tires, brakes, and steering column aside, *your eyes and vision* are the most important things to keep you from getting into an accident. In the left lane on a thruway behind a pickup full of dirt is not the time to suddenly realize you've run out of windshield wiper fluid.

Oil

You knew it was coming eventually, right? Don't worry! Checking your oil is quick and easy. If you're doing it in your driveway, don't wear good clothes, have a clean rag or paper towels with you. If the engine has been running, wait at least three minutes for the oil to drain down.

1. Make sure the car's engine is turned off and the car is parked on a level surface, with the parking brake on.
2. Open the hood and locate the oil dipstick. Do *not* confuse it with the dipsticks for transmission or steering fluid—check your manual if you're unsure.
3. Pull the dipstick out and wipe all the oil off it.
4. Put the dipstick back in and pull it out again.
5. Check where the oil level reads at the tip of the stick. Different dipsticks have different markings to indicate level.

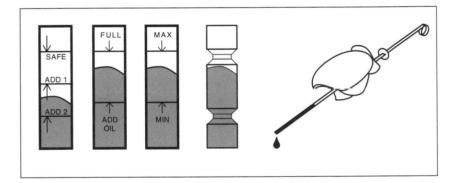

If your level shows that you're a half quart or more away from full, add oil, remembering to use the kind recommended in your owner's manual. This is where the funnel we mentioned might come in handy. Don't overfill! Add a little at a time and wait a full minute for it to drain down. Recheck your level until you're at full. If you've checked the oil and it needs more added but you're in an inconvenient spot—such as a very busy gas station—just make a note to do it when you get home.

Coolant

Of course you know by now that your car needs coolant to keep the engine operating within the right temperature range and that without enough of it your engine will overheat, possibly damaging the engine and leaving you stranded. Most cars don't use up their coolant, and you usually don't need to add more under normal driving conditions, but to be safe you should still check its level.

Never check the coolant when the engine is hot; hot coolant can cause severe burns (a strange thing, if you think about it . . .). Wait until the engine is completely cool. If you have a modern car, find the coolant reservoir and check the level there; it usually has two marks indicating maximum and minimum (or hot and cold) for proper coolant level. If the coolant is below the minimum level, you should add more, using a funnel.

If your car has no coolant reservoir, you'll have to check the level by removing the radiator cap. *Caution:* Never remove the radiator cap when the engine is warm. If you have been driving, even for one minute or so, turn off the car and wait until the engine cools completely. The hot coolant is under high pressure and can burst out and cause severe burns. Always wear eye protection and place a thick rag over the radiator cap before you unscrew it to prevent any coolant from spraying out. The coolant level should be close to the top of the radiator. If it isn't, you'll need to add more.

Be careful not to add coolant to the windshield washer fluid reservoir by mistake. Add a little at a time until you have the correct level (again with a funnel). Fill the reservoir to the minimum level. Replace the reservoir cap and run the engine for five minutes. Turn off the engine and check the level again. If more coolant is required, repeat the procedure.

Remember to use the type and mix of antifreeze and water recommended in your owner's manual—*not* what friends and family may recommend.

MONTHLY

Tires—Tread and Wear

Take a close look at your tires. Check to see that all four tires are wearing evenly and that they have a safe amount of tread. Any time a tire has less than one-sixteenth of an inch of tread left or a tread bar is showing level with two or more treads, it will require replacement. An easy way to

check this is to insert a penny head-
first into the tread: if the top of Lin-
coln's head is visible, you have less
than a sixteenth of an inch left.

Check the Brake Fluid

Brake fluid should not go down
much during normal car operation.
It doesn't hurt to check, though;

the filler should be at the top of the master cylinder. If it turns out that
you need to add fluid, you may have a brake system leak or the brake
pads might require servicing, and you should bring your car to a professional as soon as possible. Dispose of any unused brake fluid immediately; *do not* save it. An open can will absorb moisture from the air
quickly and will damage your brakes if added later on. Be careful to introduce only the recommended fluid in a brake master cylinder; other
fluids will damage the system and could cause brake failure.

Even in normal car operation, brake fluid will also attract moisture and acids that can corrode brake systems and cause problems.
Check your owner's manual: Some manufacturers recommend having
the brake fluid changed every two years—this should be done by an
expert.

Check the Power Steering Fluid

Power steering fluid is a hydraulic fluid that helps operate your steering
system. Check your owner's manual to locate where the fluid reservoir
and filler are. Again, the level shouldn't go down during normal operation, so if you're losing fluid, bring your car in ASAP. Also, just as with
brake fluid, if you wind up having to top it off, dispose of any unused
material properly.

Check the Automatic/Manual Transmission Fluid

Most manual transmission cars use transmission, or gear case oil, a
thick 70- to 120-weight gear lube, although some do use automatic
transmission fluid (check your manual). Automatic transmission cars

use—yes, you guessed it—automatic transmission fluid, or ATF. Under normal use, most cars must have the ATF or transmission oil changed at specific intervals by a professional; check your manual. In addition, check the manual for the location of the dipstick for the appropriate fluid, with a manual transmission, an inspection plug is often located *under* the car on the transmission.

Headlights, Taillights, Signal Lights

With the help of another person, check to see that all your lights are working: low beam, high beam, taillights, parking lamps, brake lights, and turn signals at all four corners. Check the hazard lights and license plate lights, too.

Less Often, but Almost as Easy

EVERY THREE MONTHS

Check the Condition of Your Air Filter

While an air filter needs to be changed at most once or twice a year, it doesn't hurt to take a look at it, especially in dusty areas. A clogged air filter can drop your mileage by a considerable percentage and wear down your engine. If you're unsure of the air cleaner's location, check your manual. It's generally very easy to remove the lid of the air cleaner, since only clamps or a wing nut hold it down. Take the filter out and hold it up to the light and tap it on the ground. Is it completely opaque? Filled with dirt and grit?

Check the Condition of the Belts

Your manual should show you where to find them under the hood (or under the car). Just keep an eye out for anything that looks as if it's wearing, fraying, or cracking, or if they look a little too shiny. (Always do this with the car off.) You usually don't need to have them replaced

more than once every four or five years, but it's a real pain when they suddenly break on the road.

Check the Condition of the Coolant Hoses in the Cooling System

While hoses need to be changed as often as belts, they're also easier to inspect. Look for collapsed or swollen hoses, holes and bulges, leaks, and oil stains. Feel them (Did we mention

the car should be off?). If they don't feel "hose-y" (i.e., cracking and brittle) or if they are giving too much, as if the material is spongy, old, and weak, it's time for a change.

Change Your Oil and Filter

All right, having your oil changed at the shop is now so cheap it almost isn't necessary for you even to think about it. But doing it yourself will give you a feeling of understanding and control over your car, at a time when there's very little left an average Joe or Josephine can tinker with on an auto.

You need:

- A socket wrench, possibly an extender bar. We're not saying that you're a ninety-pound weakling; when the car comes from the factory or has had its oil changed in a shop, professionals use wrenches to tighten the drain plug. It can be really, *really* hard for a normal human to get it off afterward.

- Oil filter wrench. Remember: This is *not* like a normal wrench. Don't think you can substitute.

- A new filter that is appropriate for your car

- A new oil pan drain plug gasket of the appropriate size

- The right oil (five to six quarts)

- Something to catch the oil in. We recommend investing in an oil catch pan, one that seals so you can bring the whole thing in for recycling. It's a lot easier than the buckets and gallon milk containers people often use.

- Work clothes, safety goggles or glasses, gloves, and clean rags

- Maybe a jack and jack stands if your car is low to the ground

1. The first thing you do is . . . yes, look at the manual. It will tell you the correct type of oil and oil filter to use, oil pan capacity, and where the oil filler, pan, and filter are if they're not immediately obvious. It might even give you a step-by-step guide to changing your oil that is far more detailed than this one.

2. Park your car on a level surface. If the car hasn't been running, start it and let it run for a few minutes before turning it off. Then wait a few more minutes so that all the oil drains back into the pan. Put on the emergency brake and place chock blocks on either side of at least two wheels.

3. With most cars, you can just crawl underneath the front end without having to lift it. We recommend this; it's easier and less dangerous if you're not used to working on cars. If you must lift the car, either use ramps (they come in pairs and are relatively inexpensive), or jack stands. Follow the instructions that come with them. *Never, ever* work under a car that's only supported by a jack!

4. Figure out where the oil pan, drain plug, and filter are. If your manual doesn't tell you and you feel at a complete loss, look for the oil filter—it will look almost exactly like the new filter you just bought. The oil pan and drain plug will be nearby. The drain plug is basically just a large nut or bolt at the bottom of the oil pan.

5. Put your oil catch pan under the drain. *Be aware that oil is hot, sticky,*

toxic, and, again, hot. From here on in be careful about splashes and spills. Put newspapers down if you're a klutz.

6. Apply the socket wrench to the drain plug and push counterclockwise. Keep your arms, face, and everything else out of the way. Be aware that unless you're fast, the drain plug will probably fall into the catch pan.

7. Let the oil drain into the pan until it's done (about ten minutes). If you want to be thorough you can wait longer until the drips stop completely (half an hour to forty-five minutes).

8. You're a third of the way done!

9. Wipe off the drain plug and reconnect it. Make sure it's screwed on tightly, but don't overtighten it and strip the plug.

10. Move the oil catch pan under the oil filter and use the filter wrench to unscrew it. Again, watch for hot, sticky oil drips. Make sure the little rubber washer (or gasket) comes off with the filter.

11. Put a little of the new oil on the new filter's gasket and make sure it's coated and rubbed in well, for a good seal. When you screw the new filter in, *do not use the filter wrench!* Only do it by hand. The instructions on the filter package will probably say something like "Tighten three-quarters of a rotation after it's on." Don't overtighten—it will damage the filter. (Some people like to write the date and mileage on the filter with a permanent marker for future reference.)

12. Okay . . . one more major task and you're done. . . .

13. Fill 'er up! Open the hood, unscrew the oil fill cap, and, using a funnel or pour spout, pour in the right amount of the right type of oil.

14. Start the engine and let it run for a few minutes. Check to see if there are any leaks from either the drain plug or the filter. Turn off the car and check the oil level again; if it needs more, top it off. Remember to put the oil filler cap back on. Now catalog the oil change in your maintenance book with date and mileage info.

15. Congratulations! Now that really wasn't so hard, was it? Whether or not you choose to do it again, at least you *can*—and you are more "in touch" with your car than before.

NOTE: Many gas stations and auto service providers like Pep Boys will take your old oil for recycling, so call around. In northern parts of the country, people sometimes have specially rigged oil burners for their house that take old car oil!

ONCE OR TWICE A YEAR
Change Your Air Filter

If you've done your three-month checks, you probably already know the condition of your filter and have changed it if it's dirty. If not, change the filter at least once or twice a year anyway—it's easy. Check your manual for the type of filter, take the old filter out, drop the new one in, and re-close the top. Really, it's that easy. Did we mention the mileage it can save you?

Check Your Cabin Filters

These filters are housed in your vehicle's air conditioner system and block potentially harmful airborne pollutants from entering the interior. It is recommended that you change your cabin air filter every 12,000 to 18,000 miles or as specified by your manufacturer.

SEASONALLY
Rotate the Tires

Rotating the tires helps them wear evenly and maximizes tread life. If you do it yourself—and we're not necessarily recommending that; it's a real pain—check your owner's manual for the order or pattern of tire rotation. If you have a full-sized spare, sometimes that gets rotated along with the others.

NOTE: The best tires should always be on the rear of the vehicle, so plan ahead and rotate them often to keep them equal!

Check the Jack

Make sure all the equipment you need to change a tire is in the car: jack, spare, lug wrench . . .

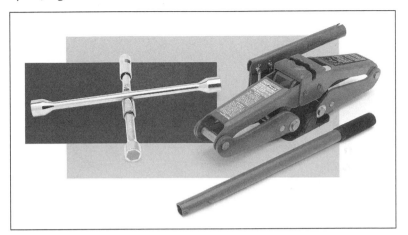

Battery Check

If you have a voltmeter/ammeter gauge in your dashboard (or know how to use a handheld one), check to see if it's showing the correct reading in the manual; otherwise, have a professional do it. If you've needed a jump start recently, have your battery and electrical system checked.

Windshield Wipers

Make sure the washers are working properly and aimed correctly: Your blades should wipe the windshield clean in two wipes. Check the wiper blades to see if they're torn or coming out of the wiper arms. If you've had problems with the blades not clearing the windshield completely, have them replaced.

Belts: A Closer Look

Check the service schedule in your owner's manual to see if the belts are scheduled for replacement, or have a technician check for you. Sometimes it's hard to tell just by looking at them if they're at the end of their life; they don't crack and fray as they age as belts used to. With the engine off, twist them so you can see the inside of the belt. This is where most of the cracking occurs on most serpentine belts.

Coolant Hoses

When the engine is cool, you or your service person can inspect them. Look for bulges, softness, and bubbles or cracking on the surface. Unfortunately, cooling hoses are generally replaced only when they break, but if your hoses are more than four years old or your engine has been overheating, it may be good insurance to have them looked at closely by a professional for replacement.

Headlights, Take Two

First, check to make sure all your lights are working, as described previously. Then make sure your headlights are aimed properly, especially if you've had trouble seeing at night recently.

1. You'll need a stretch of level pavement that extends 25 to 450 feet from a wall or garage door.
2. Pull up to three feet from the wall and put on your low beams. Outline the bright spots on the wall with chalk or tape.
3. Back up the car to twenty-five feet from the wall or door.

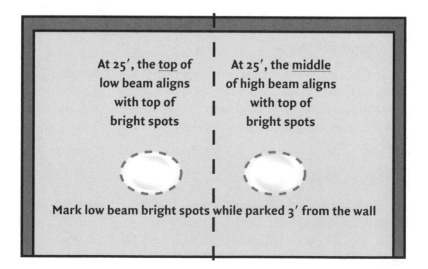

At 25', the <u>top</u> of low beam aligns with top of bright spots

At 25', the <u>middle</u> of high beam aligns with top of bright spots

Mark low beam bright spots while parked 3' from the wall

The top edge of the low beams should shine no higher than the top of the outlines on the door. The bottom edge of the low beams should shine no lower than the center of the marked outlines. For cars with four headlights, the center of the high beams should line up with the top of the outlines on the wall or door. In cars with only two headlights, the high beams are automatically aimed when the low beams are properly aimed.

If your headlights need to be adjusted, follow the instructions in your owner's manual or bring your car in for service.

Heaters, Defrosters, and Fan

These systems are not just important to maintaining a comfortable temperature—they're essential to safe driving visibility. Make sure the heater and air-conditioning are working. Check to see that the defroster/heating fan is forcing air through all the vents, with enough power to clear the window of condensate. Autumn leaves are pretty, but you still have to open the hood and clear them and any debris away from the vents at the base of the windshield.

It's also equally important that your air-conditioning works even in the winter—most cars use the AC system to dehumidify the heated air during defrost mode to eliminate windshield condensate.

If possible, test the rear defroster to make sure that all areas are being heated. If it looks as if some of the defroster wires aren't working, your service technician can sometimes repair them by applying a special conductive paint.

Exhaust System

Take a look under your car to see if any part of the exhaust seems to be hanging lower than it should. If it is, or if the exhaust has become louder or is making a different sound than it used to, have it checked. *Remember:* A faulty exhaust can potentially send fumes into the passenger area, causing sickness or death.

CAUTION: Never touch the exhaust system until it's completely cool! (We say that a lot, don't we?) Wait forty-five minutes after running the engine before touching any part of the exhaust.

Door Locks

If you drive in cold climates or use an electronic door opener you should grease your
locks with spray lubricant. If the battery
ever goes dead you'll need to get into the
car with the key.

Wash and Wax

Okay, this may seem silly and vain, but you should really wash and wax your car at least twice a year to prevent paint damage from the ele-ments—and underbody rusting from salt if you live in cold climates. Once a month would be better. And regardless of where you live, make sure you do a thorough cleaning underneath to get off the dirt. A com-plete detailing helps maintain your car's appearance longer, protecting your investment. And it will also get that funky smell out of the backseat.

Emergency Kit

If you don't have one already get one, and if you do, check it to make sure it's complete. (See the next chapter, "Safety Tips.")

Mileage Quiz

1. What's the highest mileage from a gallon of gas ever recorded for a motor vehicle?
   a) 281 miles
   b) 698 miles
   c) 9,472 miles
   d) 10,705 miles
2. Many tires have a recommended inflation range. You should keep your tire pressure:

   a) To the middle of the recommended range
   b) To the highest inflation in the range
   c) To the lowest inflation in the range
3. Underinflating your tires by 5% will drop your gas mileage by:
   a) 1%–4%
   b) 5%–10%
   c) 11%–15%
4. A clogged air filter will drop your gas mileage by:
   a) 2%
   b) 4%
   c) 6%
   d) 10%
5. Which of the following needs to be replaced regularly to make sure you maintain your car's mileage?
   a) Fuel filter
   b) Air filter
   c) PCV valve
   d) All of the above
6. What will give you better gas mileage when driving at highway speeds on a hot day?
   a) Driving with the windows down and the air conditioner off
   b) Driving with the windows up and the air conditioner on
   c) Driving with the windows halfway down and the air conditioner on
7. True or false: A loose or faulty fuel tank cap will hurt your fuel economy.
8. Driving at 75 mph rather than 65 mph increases fuel consumption by:
   a) 5%
   b) 10%
   c) 20%
   d) 25%
9. Driving with a poorly tuned engine will typically decrease fuel mileage by:
   a) 1%–4%
   b) 5%–9%
   c) 10%–20%

ANSWERS

1. The French team, Microjoule, set a new world record for fuel economy on the way to winning the 2003 Shell Eco-Marathon UK. They achieved an astounding average fuel consumption of 10,705 miles per gallon.

2. You'll always get the best gas mileage from the highest inflation in the manufacturer's recommended range.

3. You could lose 5 to 10% of your gas mileage from tires that are underinflated by as little as 5%.

4. A clogged air filter could cost you a 10% loss in mileage.

5. All these items should be replaced as part of regularly scheduled service intervals to maintain maximum gas mileage. See your vehicle's owner's manual for its recommended service schedule.

6. On most vehicles, driving with the windows up and the air conditioner on is best. The drag from having the windows open is usually more of a load on the engine than a modern automotive air-conditioning system.

7. True: Your gas could evaporate right out of the tank if the cap is not on securely.

8. At 75 miles per hour, you'll get about 25% less fuel mileage than at 65.

9. Even if it starts and runs, a poorly tuned engine could cost you 10 to 20% less miles per gallon.

CHAPTER 3

Safety Tips—Preventive and Emergency

Your Car's Emergency Kit

Yes, you need one. Even if you live in a part of the country where you're not likely to get trapped in a snowdrift for days, there are any number of other emergencies, big and small, that you will definitely want to be prepared for.

A good emergency kit should include the following:

- Jumper cables

- First-aid kit

- Tire gauge

- Road flares or warning triangles

- Nonperishable snacks (Condiment packets don't count.)

- Multi-use pocketknife

- Flashlight (Check the batteries twice a year, too.)

- Cell phone with car charger. Note: Any working cell phone can always be used to call 911 anywhere there's cell service in the United States, at no charge. You don't need an active account, and you don't need to be in your home area. So even if you don't normally own a cell phone, stash a cheap one in the glove compartment.

- Can of flat-fixing tire inflator

- Fire extinguisher

- Bottled water (Not just for you, but if your car overheats.)

- Tool kit

- Spare radiator cap

- Disposable camera (For recording details at accidents.)

- Blanket

Okay, we know what you're thinking: This stuff is *not* all going to fit in my trunk. And you're probably wondering, what is the minimum I can get away with? We don't recommend skipping on anything in this list, but if you're a mileage freak or have other reasons to keep your portage down, here are the absolute essentials:

Spare radiator cap, bottle of water, can of flat-fixing tire inflator, cell phone, jumper cables, tire gauge, multi-use pocketknife. And, obviously, a spare, a jack, and a lug wrench.

SEASONAL TRAVEL TIPS

There are things you should inspect and change about your car at the start of summer and again before winter—as well as some things you should do about your driving habits.

Winter

The first thing you should do when winter approaches is to update your emergency car kit with:

- Window scraper

- Blanket and/or extra clothes (The metallic Mylar ones fold down very compactly.)

- Spray lubricant (for door locks), the kind with the long "nose" or small plastic pipe you put over the nozzle so you can spray in tight places.

- Extra windshield washer fluid

- Shovel (You can buy folding ones.)

- Extra gloves

- Road salt

- De-icer spray

You know the whole thing about driving at least ten miles per hour slower in inclement weather, right? Here are a few other things that will make winter driving easier:

- When driving on snow or ice, it takes a lot longer to stop. Apply the brakes smoothly and begin braking sooner to avoid skids.

- Reduce your speed. Allow greater distance between you and the car in front of you. Remember: Even if you're the best ice driver in the world, the person in that car and in the one behind you probably isn't.

- Accelerate slowly to avoid skids when starting from a stop.

- Know whether you have antilock brake system brakes or not. If you do, you should brake firmly and keep firm pressure on the pedal— the ABS does the "pumping" for you. If you don't have them, you have to pump the brakes yourself to stop smoothly and safely on slick roads.

- If you drive in heavy snow, true winter tires offer much better traction than even the best "all-weather tire."

Summer

Summer means long trips to the beach or lake—as well as hot weather, lots of stop-and-go traffic, and heavy loads. The most important thing at this time of year is to keep the car from overheating.

- Don't overload. If all your passengers, luggage, pets, snorkel equipment, and random gear make your car's rear end sag, consider upgrading your shocks to maintain safe handling and braking under heavier loads.

- Towing. Many drivers who tow a trailer for the first time in hot weather don't realize the strain this puts on the engine and transmission. Tell your service technician what you'll be towing and where you're going, and ask if an additional oil cooler and transmission cooler are recommended. If your transmission fluid hasn't been changed and the car has over 60,000 miles, have this service done to ensure proper lubrication and cooling.

- *Always* test your trailer and brakes before the day of your big trip.

- Take care of the cooling system. Make sure your coolant is at the proper level, and if your engine has overheated recently, have the cooling system checked. Remember: Stop-and-go driving is actually harder on the cooling system than highway driving. Always keep an eye on the temperature gauge when you're on the road.

• Check your air conditioner. Don't wait until you're on the road in the middle of August to see if the air conditioner is working at full strength. Test it before you go. Besides keeping *you* comfortable, air conditioning can be essential to keeping the windshield fog free.

• *Never, ever* leave children or pets in a vehicle unattended, even for a minute. A locked car sitting in the sun quickly turns into an oven, with temperatures climbing from 78 degrees to 125 in as little as eight minutes.

Emergency Procedures

"Into each life some rain must fall." The trick is to understand what to do *before* any of the following things happen to you. Knowing how to handle when you have a dead battery or flat tire, when the engine over-heats, or when your brakes fail might not only save your life, it can keep your towing expenses and time spent on the side of the road to a mini-mum.

So please, read the next section *now*. You'll thank us later.

HOW TO CHANGE A FLAT TIRE

If you've been keeping an eye on your tires' wear and treads and have kept them inflated to the proper pressure, the chances of getting a flat or a blowout decrease dramatically. But sometimes you just can't avoid that screw or nail that someone thoughtfully left in the middle of the highway. Here's what to do when that happens.

First steps:

1. Drive to a safe spot well off the road so you have enough room to

work while staying clear of passing traffic. Try to park on a firm, level surface, avoiding dirt or grass if you can—your jack may sink and become unstable.

2. Turn off your engine. If you have an automatic put it in park; if your car is manual, put it in reverse. Engage the emergency or parking brakes. Get everyone out of the car.

3. Set up any emergency warning devices you might have, such as flares, flags, lights, or triangles, so drivers see them before they see you.

To fix a flat you need:

- A jack

- A jack handle or crank

- A lug wrench (On some cars, the jack handle and the wrench are combined. Lugs are the nuts that hold the wheel on—no giggling, please.)

But you already have these things in your car, because of your twice-a-year check, right?

Other things that can make the job easier:

- Screwdriver

- Rubber mallet

- Wood block

- Tire pressure gauge

- Flashlight or spotlight

- 12″ by 12″ piece of plywood to put under the jack on soft surfaces

- Work gloves

- Penetrating oil

- A large trash bag to keep the flat tire away from clean parts and tools

Okay, ready?

1. **Check your spare tire.** Make sure your spare tire is inflated properly. If it's flat (but it won't be, 'cause you check it when you check your other tires' pressure, right?), do not try to change the tire. Have your car towed. Of course, if you happen to have a portable air compressor in your trunk, you can inflate it.

   A battery-operated air compressor would also let you pump enough air into a tire with a slow leak so you can get to a service station.

2. **Loosen the lug nuts slightly— before you jack up the car.** This step is important, and it's omitted by a lot of people. Don't let anyone watching tell you different. If your car has a wheel cover or hubcap, remove it first by using a screwdriver, the flat end of the jack handle, or a lug wrench. NOTE: On some cars, the wheel cover is held in place by the lug nuts. Leave this kind in place.

   Use the lug wrench to slightly

loosen the lug nuts by turning the wrench counterclockwise. Hold the wrench firmly down. Never pull *up* on it. If the nuts are too tight, use penetrating oil to loosen them, or use your foot to push down on the lug wrench. *Loosen the lug nuts only one turn.* Do not remove the lug nuts at this time.

3. **Set up your jack.** Assemble and place your jack, following the instructions provided in your owner's manual.

Caution!

Follow these directions carefully! Placing a jack at the wrong spot can both be dangerous and damage your car. Never place the jack under an axle or suspension member.

Most cars sold in the United States are equipped with a scissors jack; it's made up of a handle and jack assembly and fits into or under special spots on the car's body. The jack is raised by turning the handle clockwise and lowered by turning the handle counterclockwise.

4. **Secure the car and jack.** Place a block of wood or a chock block under the tire diagonally opposite from the flat to prevent the car from rolling off the jack.

5. **Raise the car.** Jack up the car until the tire clears the ground. Be sure the jack stays in the correct position as you work. Remove the jack handle when you're done. Remember, *never work under a car held up by just a jack (or even two)!*

6. **Remove the lug nuts and wheel.** Use the lug wrench to remove the nuts. Place lug nuts where you won't lose them. Repeat: Place the lug nuts where you won't lose them. Pull the wheel off and set it aside.

   NOTE: Some wheels also use one "security nut" per wheel. These nuts have a special shape and require a special adapter to remove. It's usually clipped to the lug wrench or found in the glove compartment.

7. **Put on the spare.** Roll the spare into position. If necessary, jack up the car a little more to fit the spare. Make sure you have the correct side of the spare facing out (usually the label faces you). Align the wheel holes with the studs and slide the spare onto the studs. Hold the wheel in place and screw on each lug nut hand tight with the tapered end facing toward the wheel.

8. **Tighten the lug nuts.** Use the wrench to tighten the nuts following the sequence directed by your owner's manual. Otherwise, do it as shown:

   NOTE: There are different tightening sequences for four- and five-lug wheels. Tightening the nuts in the proper sequence ensures that the wheel mounts properly and that the stress is evenly distributed over the wheel.

9. **Lower the car.** Lower the jack until it's free from the weight of the car. Remove the jack and block. Tighten all nuts once more, in the proper sequence.

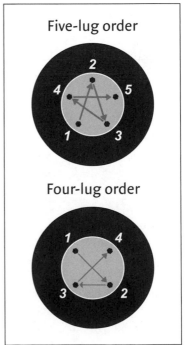

Five-lug order

Four-lug order

Caution!

Many spares are not normal, full-size tires. These smaller spares can't be driven at normal speeds and should only be driven for short distances—i.e., immediately to a service station. Consult your owner's manual for instructions and warnings for driving with a compact spare.

10. **Take the damaged tire to a service station.** Have it inspected by a professional to see if it can be repaired.

11. **Replace spare with repaired or new tire ASAP.** Check your spare's inflation and return it along with your jack and tools to their proper location.

Canned tire inflators and sealers can also provide a temporary repair for many flats without having to remove the wheel. Just remember to get to a service station immediately—and give them the can of stuff that you used. Sometimes they have to clean the gunk out of the tire afterward.

HOW TO JUMP-START YOUR ENGINE

Few things—outside of an accident or a flat tire—can make you feel more helpless and angry than putting your key in the ignition and realizing that the battery is dead, leaving you unable to get to work—or worse, stranded somewhere you don't really want to be. If you're scared of voltage and of those strange cables with the clamps thrown into the trunk of your car, relax; when done properly, starting your car from someone else's can be fast, safe, and relatively easy.

With that said . . .

Caution!

Jump-starting a dead battery is potentially dangerous if you don't know what you're doing; it must be done carefully and correctly. Failure to follow proper procedure can result in injury or death! If you think your car

isn't starting because of a dead battery, first check the *battery cables*. Cables that are loose or covered with corrosion may be the problem. Never touch the battery with bare hands! Battery acid and its byproducts *burn*. Serious injury or death can also result from the sparks and explosion that a "presumed dead" battery can generate if shorted.

1. If possible, bring the two cars together nose to nose, about eighteen inches apart. (*Not touching!*) Make sure you're parked well away from traffic, and that both cars have their parking brakes on.

2. Make sure both cars are turned off. Put automatic transmission cars in park; put manual transmission cars in neutral. Set the parking brake firmly.
3. Turn off all electrical devices in the car with the dead battery: lights, AC, radio, etc. Unplug all accessories such as cell phones or dashboard LEDs.
4. Determine which terminals are positive and negative on both bat-

teries. Look for a "+" sign or red indicator for positive, a "−" sign or black indicator for negative. But do not assume red is positive! Look for the + sign or the − sign on the battery. The positive terminal is also usually wider than the negative.

Again with the Caution!

Once you begin the next steps, do not touch the metal portion of either jumper cable clamps to those on the other one or on to any part of the car except the proper battery terminal.

5. The jumper cables are marked with the same red and black signs (positive and negative) to help you keep track of the two separate wires. Attach one end of the positive cable clamp (probably red— *not* black) to the positive terminal of the dead battery.
6. Attach the other end of the positive cable to the positive terminal of the good battery.
7. Attach one end of the negative cable to the negative terminal of the *good* battery.

Caution, Take Three!

YOUR CABLES ARE NOW LIVE! DO NOT TOUCH THE REMAINING CABLE CLAMP'S METAL PORTION TO YOURSELF.

8. Attach the other end of the negative cable to a metal section (bracket, block, etc.) of the engine away from any moving parts (belts and pulleys can be dangerous once your engine is up and running). Connecting this cable last and away from the battery will avoid sparks and other potential hazards. You may see a small spark when you attach this end—this is normal. If it is a large spark, disconnect immediately and check to make certain the black cable is on the negative (−) terminal.
9. Make sure everyone is clear of the engine compartment in each car—don't allow hands or clothing to be caught by moving engine parts.
10. Start the engine of the good car. Allow it to run for one to two minutes. Rev the engine a bit by lightly tapping the gas pedal.
11. Start the engine of the dead car. If it does not crank check the con-

nections and let it charge again. It may take more than one try, but don't do it more than three or four times.

Once Again: Caution!

Some cars' electrical and computer systems may be damaged by running the engine with a dead battery. Check your owner's manual or service provider for guidance.

If the Car Still Won't Start

If the dead car still doesn't make a click when you turn the key, the jumper cables may not have a good connection at the battery terminals. Turn off both engines and try rocking the cable clamps back and forth to get them to really dig in (watch your hands). Also try another ground point to attach the negative cables. Retry from step 9.

That Didn't Do It?

If the car still won't start, allow the good car to run for five to ten minutes while hooked up to the dead car. Rev the engine slightly. This may build a charge in the dead battery and allow you to restart.

Okay. Time to Give Up.

If these steps don't work after three or four more tries, *stop trying*. The battery may be shorted internally, or the dead car may have other electrical issues besides the battery. Continuing at this point could cause damage to the electrical system—have your car towed.

WHAT TO DO WHEN YOUR BRAKES FAIL

Modern brake systems are extremely reliable, and a sudden loss of all braking power is very rare, especially if you've kept your car tuned up and followed your manual's service schedule. But it doesn't hurt to know what to do ahead of time so you don't panic if the unlikely does occur.

Very quickly, try the following three things:

1. **Pump the brakes.** Sometimes pumping the brake pedal rapidly several times will generate enough braking power to stop.
2. **Apply the parking brake.** Do it gradually. Be aware that applying it suddenly can cause the car to skid.
3. **Try downshifting.** With an automatic transmission, carefully shift from D into 3, then 2, then 1. With a manual transmission, downshift from the higher to lower gears one at a time. Remember our early discussion about how you can have either power or speed in a car? Downshifting uses the resistance of the engine to slow the car.

Once you're able to slow the car, steer toward the shoulder of the road and try to pull off into a safe area. Put on your emergency flashers to let other drivers know you're having trouble.

Even if these steps helped you to stop successfully, *don't try to drive the car again.* Get help immediately and have the car towed.

WHAT TO DO WHEN YOUR ENGINE OVERHEATS

Most of the time when your engine overheats, it's not a spectacular, movie-quality explosion of steam underneath your hood. This is a good thing   because that would mean your hoses have blown (or something worse), and you need to be towed.

If you've kept up your coolant levels and dutifully checked the state of the hoses, overheating is far, *far* less likely to occur. But even the best maintained vehicle can give up its ghost in bumper-to-bumper traffic on the way to the beach in mid-August.

1. The best thing you can do is try to *avoid* a complete meltdown by keeping an eye on your temperature gauge. If the needle starts climbing dangerously high and it is easy to do so, get off the road and park someplace safe where the car can cool down.
2. If you missed this sign, the car is overheating, and it's not convenient for you to pull over, turn your air conditioner off. Yup, it's a painful step, but at least you can open the windows.
3. If the car is *still* overheating, you have to suffer through far worse to save your car: Turn your heater and fan on full blast. Remember how earlier you learned that the passenger area of the car is heated with some of the leftover heat the engine produces? By turning the

heater and fan on you are actively diverting more heat out of the engine and into the passenger area, taking the load off it.

4. If your passengers complain, remind them that driving a car that's overheated can damage it badly, and pretty much immediately. Metal melts, remember?

5. If it's *still* overheating, pull the car over immediately and turn it off.

6. Once it's cooled down some, pop open the hood. If there's no steam spraying out, it's probably not a burst hose. If it is a burst hose, call for a tow truck and do *not* drive your car.

7. Is the radiator pressure cap still on? If not, you have a replacement one in your trunk—right?

8. If the cap is still on, check the coolant level in the reserve—(CAUTION!) *remembering that if you fill the radiator directly (not a reservoir), you must let the engine cool down* completely *before taking off the radiator cap.* Hot coolant spraying out will be painful.

9. If the coolant level is low, first check for leaks under the car. If there are no leaks or only a small one, you can use the bottle of water you keep in the trunk to top off the coolant. Just remember to have the whole coolant system flushed and refilled as soon as you get back— your car really needs the mix of water with antifreeze.

10. If nothing else seems wrong, wait forty-five minutes for the car to cool down. If it starts and runs at its normal temperature, you can drive merrily off, but keep a closer eye on the needle this time. Remember to have it checked out completely. Something caused it to overheat and it will do it again if you ignore the warnings!

WHAT TO DO IN AN ACCIDENT

We hope you never have to deal with this, but if you're a regular commuter or drive as much as the average American, there's a pretty good chance you're going to be in one sooner or later—remember, other people can cause accidents, too. It's not just you.

The most important thing is to keep calm and rational. Running around in the street, waving your arms at traffic and screaming, isn't going to do anyone any good.

1. Stop the car if it's still moving and pull off the road or as far away from it as you can.

2. Try to get all the other cars and people involved safely off the road as well—if the cars are too damaged, leave them there but put your warning flares, triangles, etc., around them.
3. *Do not leave the scene of the accident.*
4. Check to see the condition of everyone involved. If anyone is injured—even the slightest bit—call 911 and then the police.
5. If it was a hit-and-run—even if no one was injured—call the police.
6. And now the part most people don't remember: collecting details.
   - First, your own:
     - Location, date, and time of accident
   - The other driver(s):
     - Name, address, license number, and telephone number
     - Insurance company and policy number—phone number, if you can
     - Make, model, year of other car or cars involved, and license plate numbers

   NOTE: If the driver of a car is not the same as the *owner* of the car, you must get the insurance and contact information of the actual owner as well.

   NOTE: You must share all of this same information about you to anyone else involved in the accident!

   - The police officer:
     - Name, phone number, badge number, incident or report number
   - Witnesses:
     - Names, addresses, and phone numbers. Remember, these are people completely uninvolved with the accident—*not* passengers.
7. In addition, jot down anything else you feel was significant to the accident: weather, time of day, how you remember it occurring, which way each of the cars was going, etc. Draw a diagram if you can, while your memory is still fresh.
8. Take a picture with the disposable camera you keep in your glove compartment of everything relevant to the accident, primarily car damage.
9. When talking to the police officer, be polite and objective. Stick to

the facts, ma'am—do not accuse anyone of anything. Also, unfortunately, do not tell anyone you're sorry or that it was your fault. It might not have been, and you want the law and the insurance companies to treat you fairly later on.

10. If your car is damaged, get it towed to a service station. Remember to keep all receipts and call the other driver's insurance company as soon as you get home.

11. If you have been injured even a little bit, notify the police officer at the scene and go to the doctor immediately to get a complete checkup. Some things that might not seem serious (ringing in the ears, nausea, etc.) can turn out to be *very* serious.

12. Get copies of the police record, any medical receipts or reports, and anything else that pertains to the accident.

13. Don't sign anything that isn't provided to you by the police, your lawyer, or your own insurance agency.

IF YOU'RE STRANDED BY YOURSELF ON THE SIDE OF THE ROAD:

If you think these precautions are silly, go out and rent a copy of *Deliverance*.

First off, use the cell phone you keep in your glove compartment and call 911.

If you're out of range, open your hood—it's the international symbol for a broken-down car. Someone will notice it.

If it's at night and you're safely off the road, stay in your car. Keep the windows mostly up and the doors locked. If someone stops to offer help, *ask them to call someone for you,* and do *not* get out of the car. If the person claims he's a police officer—and he doesn't come in a police car—thank him politely and repeat that you would like him to call for help—*other* help.

And while we're on this subject . . . if you have a hands-free cell phone and happen to drive by someone stranded, call 911 for them.

CHAPTER 4

Service and Repair

Unfortunately, there's a limit to what even a skilled home technician can do for his or her car; that's where taking your car in for service comes in.

Understanding the Service Schedule

Remember how we told you to check in the owner's manual for your car's service schedule?

For now, you can read along with this one and we'll break it down into what each kind of service means.

Service Description	Recommended Maintenance/Inspection Intervals*
Headlights & Small Bulbs	Check Weekly
Lube and Oil Filter	3,000 Miles/3 Months
Battery	6,000-Mile Inspection

*These recommendations are suggested only to maximize the safety, efficiency, and longevity of your vehicle. They are based on the "severe service or use" of your vehicle. Your vehicle manufacturer's recommendation and warranty requirements may differ. Consult your owner's manual for additional information.

CV Boots	6,000-Mile Inspection
Tire Rotation	6,000 Miles
Wheel Alignment	6,000-Mile Inspection
Air Filter	12,000-Mile Inspection
Breather Filter	12,000-Mile Inspection
Canister Filter	12,000-Mile Inspection
Cooling System Service	12,000 Miles/12 Months
Emission Service	12,000-Mile Inspection
Engine Analysis	12,000-Mile Inspection
Engine Tune-Up (Non-Computer)	12,000 Miles
Exhaust Parts	12,000-Mile Inspection
Fuel Filter (Carburetor)	12,000 Miles
Fuel Filter (Injection)	12,000 Miles
PCV Valve	12,000 Miles/24 Months
Shock Absorbers	12,000-Mile Inspection
Steering Parts	12,000-Mile Inspection
Struts & Cartridges	12,000-Mile Inspection
Wheel Bearings	
Repack Seals (Non Drive Axle)	12,000 Miles
Wiper Blades	12,000-Mile Inspection
Air-Conditioning Service	24,000 Miles/24 Months
Brakes	24,000-Mile Inspection
CV Joints	24,000-Mile Inspection
Drive Axle Bearings & Seals	24,000-Mile Inspection
Engine Tune-Up (Computer)	24,000 Miles
Fan/Accessory Belts	24,000 Miles
Fuel Injector Cleaning	24,000 Miles
Power Flush Cooling System	24,000 Miles
Suspension Parts	24,000-Mile Inspection
Transmission Service	24,000 Miles/24 Months
Oxygen Sensor	30,000-Mile Inspection
Cooling System Hoses	36,000 Miles/36 Months
Universal Joints	36,000-Mile Inspection
Vacuum Modulator	36,000 Miles/36 Months
Timing Belts	60,000 Miles/48 Months

Yours will probably look a little different, with a table consisting of service required, what needs to be performed (inspected or actually worked on) and then an interval number—such as every 3,000 miles or every three months, every 12,000 miles or every year. Often it will just say miles or km × 1000, or months, like this:

Service	Months	3	12	30
	Miles × 1000	3	20	30
	KM × 1000	4.8	32	48
Oil change		D	D	D
Disc brakes and pads			X	
Spark plugs				R

In this case, "D" = Do (an oil change)
   "X" = Have the part examined (sometimes it's I for inspected)
   "R" = Have the part replaced

The way to read this is that *every* 3,000 miles or three months, including at 6,000, 9,000, 12,000, 15,000, 30,000, etc., miles, you must Do an oil change. Every 20,000 miles (including 40,000 and 60,000, etc.) you should have your brakes Examined (or sometimes I for Inspected), and the spark plugs should be Replaced *every* 30,000 miles.

You may note that at many of the bigger mileages—like 30,000—a lot of these inspections and routine replacements occur at the same time. In fact with many cars, the "big" services come at 30,000, 60,000, and 90,000 miles (or 15, 24, and 60 months—whatever your manual dictates). Do not skip *anything* on your schedule. Besides keeping your car running well for the long haul, it will make it a lot easier to sell for more money if and when you decide to do so.

WHAT THE DIFFERENT SERVICES MEAN

By now you shouldn't have any problem understanding how or why a particular part of your car needs to be inspected or replaced; you know that disc pads wear out, that fluids lose their ability to lubricate or cool, and that it's difficult to inspect your own spark plugs.

Many of the things you see on the example schedule, and possibly in your own service schedule (such as breather filter, PCV valves, oxygen sensor, etc.), are items that only a heavy do-it-yourselfer or technician can inspect and/or replace and that don't require you to make any decisions or necessarily have a thorough understanding of the part. An oxygen sensor, for example, senses how much oxygen is coming out of the engine and updates the car's computer to change the gas/air mixture, if necessary. A technician will check to see if it is working properly, and replace it for you if it isn't. Same with spark plugs—engine access is often too tight to allow you to inspect and replace them yourself much anymore.

There are, however, details you should know about what goes on when a professional services the major car systems, so you can know ahead of time what questions to ask or what choices you will need to make. Some of the explanations here on how parts of your car can go bad or need to be adjusted may seem a little dull. Read it anyway—and not right before your car needs to be serviced!

SUSPENSION PARTS: SHOCKS/STRUTS

While you should pay attention to how the car drives, the shocks and/or struts can experience wear that you may not notice. For the health of your car and your own driving safety, they should be inspected thoroughly by a technician while the car is on a lift. Worn shocks and struts don't keep your tires on the road as well, making it much harder to stop, steer, and safely drive down the road.

Signs That Your Shocks May Need Service:

- Car rides rougher or much softer
- Car keeps bouncing several times after you hit a bump
- You hear clunking or banging when you hit bumps or potholes
- Car doesn't steer as well
- Car bottoms out over bumps or when heavily loaded
- You see fluid leaking from a shock or strut
- Car dips to one side as you drive or when braking

- Car rolls or sways excessively when cornering

- The front of the car dips down severely when braking

- Your tires are wearing out in a choppy fashion

In most cases worn shocks and struts can't be rebuilt—they can only be replaced (except for a few early strut-equipped vehicles that allow you to replace the strut cartridge only). If you have struts replaced that have more than 40,000 miles on them, it's a good idea to have the strut mounts replaced as well; they are generally equipped with bearings and are important for proper alignment and steering.

Sometimes people change their shocks or struts to change the way their car rides. If you think the ride is too hard you can put on "softer" units to make the ride smoother. If your car leans too much while turning or "nose-dives" while braking, you can put on "stiffer" units to improve the handling. If you tow a trailer or often carry heavy loads, it may be a good idea to have different shocks from the ones your car came with. The most common types of shocks are as follows:

- **Standard.** The ones that came with your vehicle were probably chosen for a good compromise of handling, comfort, and cost under normal driving conditions.

- **Heavy duty.** These are designed for handling heavier loads or towing a trailer. They are usually "stiffer" than standard shocks and give better control at higher speeds and on rough roads.

- **High-performance gas shocks and struts.** These are designed to improve handling at high speeds and hard acceleration. They can deliver a stiffer ride but help keep the car level in fast turns and during hard braking.

- **Overload shocks.** These have a spring on the outside that helps them handle very heavy loads. They're typically used for towing or on off-road vehicles.

- **Air shocks.** By changing the pressure in these, drivers can adjust their ride for a very wide range of loads. They're used most often in vehicles that tow heavy trailers (and occasionally luxury cars, to give a better combination of handling and comfort). The shocks are inflated either by a standard air pump or an on-board air compressor system.

- **Adjustable.** By making an adjustment on the exterior of the unit, these shocks and struts can be tuned to a smoother ride or better handling. However, even on their softest setting most adjustable shocks can be stiffer than standard ones.

- **Coil-over shocks.** Designed for extreme high-performance driving, these are true racing-style shocks—and therefore appropriately expensive. They must be carefully matched to the specific car and should only be installed by a professional.

- **Monotube.** Traditional shocks have two tubes: Fluid travels between the inner and outer tubes to control shock movement (think of those desktop executive toys that you tip to watch blue goo flow slowly against the water and into a funnel or hole or whatever). Monotubes have only one tube, and it's filled with shock fluid plus a high-pressure gas. In general, they provide a better combination of handling and comfort than "twin tube" shocks.

- **Self-adjusting.** Many of today's better shocks are designed to adapt instantly to road conditions. These feature special valves that stiffen shock responses when the wheel travels over potholes and bumps. This helps to maintain handling and braking, but allows a comfortable ride on smooth roads.

WHEEL ALIGNMENT

When your car was designed, the manufacturer calculated the ideal position for the wheels in relation to the car so you could get the best possible control, comfort, tire life, and fuel economy. Your car is out of alignment when the wheels come out of their correct positions. Misalignment accelerates tire wear as well as affecting your braking and handling and—in essence, your ability to control your car in emergencies and on slick roads.

Often an inspection of your alignment won't show up on a service schedule—it's something you request when you notice certain symptoms and you're certain it's not *tire pressure*.

Signs That You Need Your Alignment Checked

A change of handling is the main clue: your steering wheel is crooked on a straight road or your car tends to drift to one side when driving on a straight and level road, or if you have to hold the steering wheel tightly to keep the car moving straight ahead.

When you check your tires, uneven wear is another clue that your alignment needs to be checked (*see chart on page* 84).

NOTE: Uneven tire wear can also be caused by a wheel that's bent or out of balance. Whenever you have your car aligned, have your technician check the balance on all four wheels.

NOTE TOO: *Uneven* tire pressure can also have the same effect as your wheels being out of alignment. Before you spend beaucoup bucks to have your wheels aligned, check your tires with a good-quality gauge you have on hand (right?) to make sure they have the correct pressure, according to your car manual. *If this doesn't fix the problems,* then go see a technician.

Hitting a deep pothole or curb are two common causes of misalignment. Any hard impact to the wheels or collision (even a minor one) can cause it also. Age loosens parts and creates sag in the front frame section and normal wear and tear on your suspension components may also contribute to misalignment.

Things to be aware of when having your car aligned:

- If no suspension parts are damaged, loose, or worn, a simple adjustment will do (few $$$).

- If the parts *are* loose, worn, or damaged, they may have to be replaced before a proper wheel alignment can be performed (a little more $$$).

- Some alignment settings may not have factory adjustments. If these get knocked out, you may require aftermarket "shims" or "eccentrics" to repair the problem (slightly more $$$).

- Cars that have had their body or frame bent in an accident may never be brought back into proper alignment. In this case, technicians will try to align the wheels in the correct position or in relation to one another, if not the car itself (much more $$$).

- Any time you buy new tires, get your car aligned. The cost is small compared to the price of the new tires and will help you get the most mileage possible.

- Alignments require specialized equipment and should be done by trained specialists.

BATTERY

You just never think about them until the car won't start.

Your battery's life depends on the type of battery, where you live, your car type, and how you drive. Typically today's batteries can be expected to last from three to five years under average conditions and proper use. Extremely cold or hot weather, frequent short trips, and constantly running accessories when the engine is off will wear them out sooner. Electrical system problems such as a faulty alternator can keep the battery from recharging properly.

But *all* batteries wear out eventually (i.e., they no longer hold a charge) and have to be replaced. Some modern batteries have indicators on them that tell you if they are fully charged: green if it's fully charged and black if it has lost its charge. Always have the battery checked when your service schedule suggests, and replaced if it's worn out—but *have the entire electrical system* checked out by a technician first. A brand-new battery can be discharged if it's put into a car with an electrical system problem (and an alternator can be damaged if the vehicle is run with a dead battery for an extended period of time).

If you're going to replace the battery yourself, bring the old one into the shop—they will properly dispose of it for you.

If you're just having a routine inspection done (no symptom of any sort), the technician will suggest cleaning the terminals of any corrosion or white powder and covering it with a protectant, as well as using a computer to test the starter, alternator, and regulator and seeing if there's a "parasitic draw" of electricity from the system by a faulty component.

BRAKES

Brakes *work* by friction and will eventually wear out! All disc brakes will need their pads replaced, and drum brakes will need their shoes replaced. After enough miles the rotors and drums may need to be resurfaced ("cut" or "turned"), but eventually they will need complete replacement. It's not always obvious when you should do that. As they wear out it may take longer for your car to stop, but because it's gradual you may not notice anything. That's why it's important to stick to the service schedule—even if nothing seems wrong. It's a good idea to have your service technician take a look at them every time your car is in for service, since it's already up on the lift.

Many cars require that their brakes be inspected and brake fluid replaced every ten or fifteen thousand miles. A technician will go in and closely examine and measure the brake lines, attaching hardware, brake drums or discs, and brake shoes or pads. If either of the last two are wearing thin they will be required to be replaced to bring the system back to specifications.

Signs That It's Time to Bring Your Car In for a Brake Inspection

Major Problems:

- Suddenly you're unable to stop normally

- The brake pedal suddenly goes all the way to the floor or feels very mushy

- The brake pedal feels very hard and high

- The brake fluid is very low (could indicate a leak)

- Severe squealing or scraping noises

- Pulling very hard to one side

If you experience any of these symptoms, *pull over immediately* and have your car towed to a service station. *Do not drive* to a garage; you could lose control of your car.

Signs That It's Time for (Less Immediate) Brake Service

- Vibration or pulsation in the pedal when you lightly apply the brakes—and your brakes *aren't* antilock

- Needing to pump the brakes several times to get stopping power

- Brakes lose power after several stops

- Brakes don't stop as well as they used to

- Car pulls slightly to one side when braking

- Brake light comes on and *stays* on, or comes on while you're driving

- Brake fluid is slightly low

- Scraping, grinding, or groaning noises when you apply the brakes

About the scraping, squealing, grinding, or groaning:

You might hear these noises just after going through a car wash or the first time you hit the brakes after going through a puddle. This is normal and should go away after you make a few stops.

If you hear a *slight* squealing right after the brakes have been serviced, it's probably a high-frequency vibration caused by new pads (or shoes) mating to the rotors (or drum). This noise usually goes away as the pads wear evenly—sometimes your technician can use antisqueal parts or chemicals to help make it stop.

Some brakes have wear indicators that are designed to make noise when service is required. See above re: taking your car in to have the brakes checked.

In any case, if your brakes make loud noises and don't stop very well it *probably* means that you require new pads, shoes, and/or other brake work. Get it taken care of right away. Replacing worn pads or shoes is relatively inexpensive, but continuing to drive with them can damage the rotors or drums—which is way, *way* more expensive.

And did we mention that it's dangerous, too?

TIRES

Tires can last anywhere between 20,000 and 80,000 miles depending on what kind they are, your car, how you drive, how often you rotate your tires, and the roads you travel. When it comes time to replace one, do all four. Do not mix and match tires. Doing so can create problems in handling and braking.

A good way to remember when and how to service them is PART:

- **Pressure.** You can check this regularly yourself. Look on your car doorjamb or owner's manual for the correct pressures—not on the tire! That number is the max pressure the tire will handle properly.

- **Alignment.** Have your service technician check the alignment periodically, and always after an especially bad jolt from hitting a curb or going over a pothole.

- **Rotation.** Do it (or have it done) when your owner's manual recommends, or we recommend every 6,000 to 8,000 miles.

- **Tread.** Use the chart on the next page if you notice anything unusual during your "at the pump" visual inspections.

AIR FILTER

You do that yourself now, right? The checking and replacing?

LUBE/OIL AND FILTER CHANGE

Most service centers—like Pep Boys—will include a lot of other minor inspections with this service, such as checking the air filter, the coolant level, tire pressure, etc. Remember to specify if you want normal, high mileage, or synthetic oil.

COOLANT INSPECTION, FLUSH, AND CHANGE

The technician can "take a reading" (just like Mr. Spock) of how weak your coolant is, and whether it should be topped off or completely replaced. As with an oil change, they first drain it all out and then add new coolant, according to the type recommended in your owner's manual. At the same time the technician will probably (read: *should*):

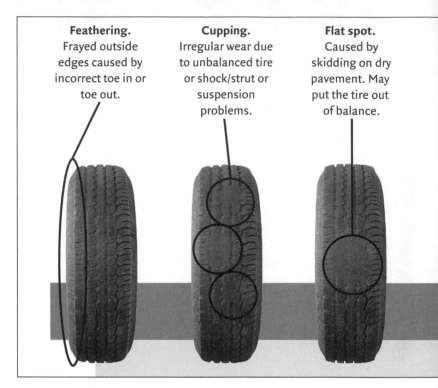

Feathering. Frayed outside edges caused by incorrect toe in or toe out.

Cupping. Irregular wear due to unbalanced tire or shock/strut or suspension problems.

Flat spot. Caused by skidding on dry pavement. May put the tire out of balance.

- Do a visual check of the cooling system for indications of leaks or oil content.

- Pressure test the entire cooling system and radiator cap.

- Test the coolant thermostat with a radiator thermometer.

- Check the temperature gauge for accuracy.

- Clean up the radiator fins, if needed.

- Check fan blades and pulleys for alignment and damage.

- Inspect all hoses for cracks, swelling, brittleness, and deterioration (but you've been keeping an eye on that, right?), as well as all belts and the water pump. Replace the hoses and hose clamps, if necessary—or at the time suggested in the service manual. Do not wait for them to blow, new engines damage very quickly when overheated!

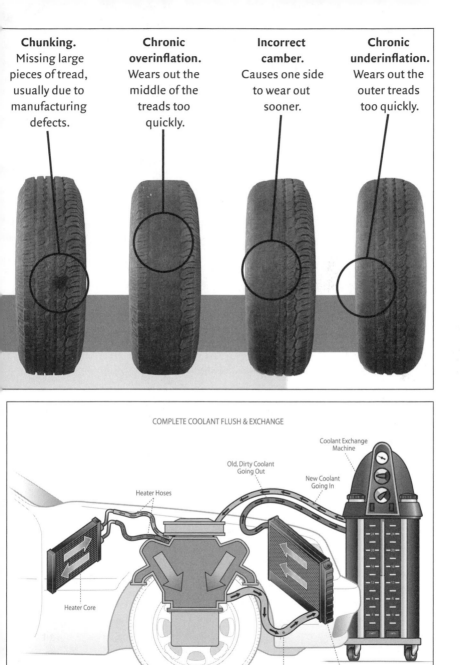

Chunking. Missing large pieces of tread, usually due to manufacturing defects.

Chronic overinflation. Wears out the middle of the treads too quickly.

Incorrect camber. Causes one side to wear out sooner.

Chronic underinflation. Wears out the outer treads too quickly.

COMPLETE COOLANT FLUSH & EXCHANGE

Coolant Exchange Machine

Old, Dirty Coolant Going Out

New Coolant Going In

Heater Hoses

Heater Core

Lower Radiator Hose

Radiator

THE "BIG" SERVICES

Whether it's at 30,000, 60,000, or 90,000 miles (or whatever your service schedule recommends), here is what you can expect to be done on your car, and what you should keep track of in your repair notebook:

- All the belts should be inspected and possibly replaced: camshaft, timing belt, alternator, fanbelt, power steering, etc.

- All the filters should be inspected and possibly replaced: oil, fuel, air, breather, cabin, etc.

- All fluids should be checked and topped-off or replaced: oil, coolant, brake, transmission, power steering, differential, etc.

- The entire brake system should be inspected and parts replaced if worn beyond specs or broken: brake lines, pads, shoes, parking brake, hardware, etc.

- Steering, suspension, and alignment should all be checked, adjusted, and broken or worn parts replaced

- All of the spark plugs should be replaced

- The universal joints, whether CV or driveshaft, should be inspected

- Wiper blades should be inspected and replaced

- Air-conditioning system inspected

- Battery tested, cleaned, and replaced if necessary

- All wire connections inspected

- All gaskets, seals, bushings, etc., inspected, treated if possible, and replaced if old and cracked

- Bearings inspected and lubricated

- Emissions/exhaust inspected

- A computer tune-up analysis. This means two things: 1) They check to see how well all the electronic/computer parts of your car work, from the fuel injection sensors to self-adjusting shocks if your car has them; 2) They actually *use* a computer to diagnose a lot of your car's problems that would normally be hard to notice.

- Fuel injectors and throttle body inspected, cleaned, and chemical added to the tank to clean all of them

Expect to spend a fair amount of money on these checkups, and to have them a little more often if you drive under what your manual considers "severe conditions." Do *not*, however, skip *any* of them. That will shorten the life of your car and lower considerably its resale value.

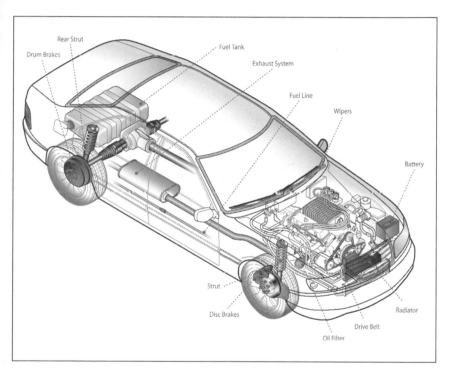

Table of Symptoms

This is a basic list of symptoms and their probable causes, so you can either figure out what it is yourself or be able to eliminate some of the possibilities when speaking to your technician.

If . . .	SHOCKS STRUTS SUSPENSION PARTS	ALIGNMENT	TIRE ISSUES: BALANCE OR PRESSURE	BATTERY	ALTERNATOR	BRAKES	HOSES	NOTES:
Car rides rougher	X							
Car keeps bouncing several times after you hit a bump	X							
You hear clunking or banging when you hit bumps or potholes	X							Exhaust/ tail pipe
Car doesn't steer as well	X	X	X					
Car bottoms out over bumps or when heavily loaded	X							
Car vibrates at higher speeds		X	X					
Car pulls to one side as you drive or when braking	X	X	X			X		
Car rolls or sways excessively when cornering	X							
The front of the car dips down severely when braking	X							
Your tires are wearing out unevenly	X	X	X					
Steering wheel remains crooked on a straight road		X	X					
Car drifts to one side on a straight and level road		X	X					
You have to hold steering wheel tightly to keep car moving straight		X	X					
Car needs to be jump-started often				X	X			Accessory left on?

If . . .	SHOCKS STRUTS SUSPENSION PARTS	ALIGNMENT	TIRE ISSUES: BALANCE OR PRESSURE	BATTERY	ALTERNATOR	BRAKES	HOSES	NOTES:
Suddenly you're unable to stop in your normal distance						X		Pull the car over and have it towed to a service station immediately.
The brake pedal suddenly goes all the way to the floor or feels very mushy						X		
The brake pedal feels very hard and high						X		
You hear: scraping, grinding, or groaning noises when you apply the brakes						X		Get your car serviced as soon as you can.
You feel: vibration or pulsation in the pedal when you apply the brakes—and your brakes *aren't* antilock						X		
You need to pump the brakes several times to get stopping power						X		
The brakes lose power after several stops						X		
Brake fluid is very low or leaking from the car						X		
Brakes don't stop as well as they used to						X		Get your car serviced as soon as you can.
There's uneven tire wear	X	X	X					
A piece of electrical equipment doesn't work								Check for a blown fuse first.
Bad gas mileage		X	X					Check air filter.
Knocking/Pinging								Wrong octane

If . . .	SHOCKS STRUTS SUSPENSION PARTS	ALIGNMENT	TIRE ISSUES: BALANCE OR PRESSURE	BATTERY	ALTERNATOR	BRAKES	HOSES	NOTES:
Car won't start				X	X			Starter could also be dead.
Battery frequently dies				X	X			
Engine overheats							X	Check radiator cap and coolant level, too.

How to Tell What's Leaking

Color	Probable Fluid
Clear	Water Most likely condensation from the air conditioner, generally found under the middle of the vehicle on the right side. Don't worry! Note: on some cars, air conditioners run whenever the defroster is used.
Usually green or greenish blue, slimy and slightly sweet-smelling. Can also be bright pink or orange.	Coolant (anti-freeze) From the overflow, radiator or a leak in the system.
Bright blue, no smell	Windshield washer fluid
Amber to black, oily	Engine oil
Amber to light brown, oily	Power steering fluid
Reddish pink, oily	Automatic transmission fluid
Almost clear to light brown or reddish brown, oily	Brake fluid
Black/brown, oily	Differential oil

LIGHTS, GAUGES, AND DIALS

Don't ignore them. And don't say, "Oh, that comes on all the time. It doesn't mean anything." The warning lights and gauges on your dashboard really *can* tell you when your engine is headed for trouble.

When you first turn on your car all the warning lights will come on briefly. If any of them stay on or come on *while your engine is running* it means there is a problem (if nothing else, that the light is broken).

		What it means
CHECK BRAKES	**Brake System /ABS**	This light tells you that your parking brake is on or that you may have trouble with your brakes or ABS system. If this light stays on after you start driving or comes on *while* you're driving, have your brakes checked immediately. It could mean brake failure is imminent.
[+ −] **ALT**	**Charging System**	If this light stays on after you start, it means that your battery isn't being charged and you need to have your electrical system checked. You may be running your battery down, and your engine might stop while you're driving, or you may be unable to restart your car after you have stopped.
OIL	**Engine Oil Pressure**	If this light stays on after you start driving or comes on while you're driving, you need to check your oil. Pull off the road as soon as possible and follow the instructions in the "Basic Car Care Maintenance" chapter or your owner's manual for checking and adding oil. Do *not* run your engine if this light stays on—low oil pressure can severely damage your engine.

		What it means
CHECK ENGINE	Check Engine/ Service Soon	The "Check Engine Light" on OBD II cars (1994 and newer) is designed to monitor the performance of the emissions systems and components and goes on when it detects failures in these systems. If your engine light is on, it could mean problems with your emissions system or engine controls. If this light stays on after you start or comes on while you're driving, have your car checked out as soon as possible. Don't drive long distances or to a place where it will be hard to get towing or service.
	Water Temperature Gauge	Some cars have gauges as well as warning lights. All cars have a water temperature gauge. Keep an eye on the engine temperature every time you drive. It's normal for the gauge to go a little above normal and then come back down a bit. However, if the needle goes into the "hot" area on the gauge, pull over as soon as safely possible and turn the engine off—your engine is overheating and can be severely damaged if you keep driving. Wait until the engine cools and check to see if you have enough coolant; if you do, you may have some other engine problem. Have your car towed to a garage for service—but *do not* drive it again.
	Other Engine Gauges	Some cars have other gauges that show things such as oil level, oil pressure, and electrical flow. If you're not sure what one is . . . read your owner's manual!

CHAPTER 5

Appearance and Accessories

Improving Your Car's Appearance and Performance

Now for the fun stuff!

(You didn't skip ahead to this part, did you?)

At the beginning of this book you probably thought of auto parts and accessories stores (such as Pep Boys) as big, scary places that smell of rubber and oil, full of little boxes of things that you didn't really understand. Now that you know better, go and take another walk down the aisles. Check out the different kinds of oil you can buy, the additives that do different things, and the fantastic tools that you can outfit your garage with.

Additives

Today there are many different kinds of additives available designed to help maximize your car's performance and help it last longer. Each one is formulated to do a specific job, so it's important to know the difference between them. Read the labels carefully and follow the manufacturer's directions—*after* checking your owner's manual to make sure they're approved for your car.

When you read about what each of the additives do, try to imagine the car system it's for and figure out why it works. For instance, why *would* a fuel injector cleaner help with your car's acceleration and power? Answer: because fuel injectors are what fill the cylinder with gas for the explosion—if they get all gummed up, they can't shoot out as much fuel or as fast, which means smaller, more badly timed explosions.

FUEL ADDITIVES

These are designed to help improve engine performance and clean the fuel system and maintain mileage efficiency.

- **Octane boosters** increase the effective (surprise!) octane of gas to help increase power and help prevent knocks and pings. Higher octane provides a smoother running engine and better acceleration. These additives are primarily recommended for high-performance engines, so it's important to read the label carefully. The type of fuel that you use will determine the performance of the additive.

- **Gas treatments and fuel systems cleaners** are designed to help clean deposits in the fuel system (*duh*) and enable the detergents already in your gasoline to work better. By cleaning the fuel injectors, intake valves, and combustion chambers, these products help improve engine power.

- **Fuel injector cleaners** remove gum, varnish, and carbon buildup in today's highly sensitive fuel injectors, helping to maintain your car's power and acceleration.

- **Carburetor cleaners** are for older cars, and are usually a blend of solvents that are *sprayed on* carburetors, linkages, and choke assemblies. They help remove varnish, dirt, lead, and carbon deposits and help restore performance, smooth idling, and improve acceleration.

- **Fuel antifreeze/water removers** are added to gasoline to help prevent ice buildup and gas line freezing. They also help eliminate moisture that can condense in the gas itself, which is especially useful for cars with starting problems in cold weather.

• **Fuel stabilizers.** Gasoline is supposed to be used within one to three months of refining; these additives are designed to help prevent gasoline from breaking down into tars and varnish that will gum up the fuel system and make it difficult to start the engine next time. Stabilizers are particularly useful if you have an RV, lawn mower, chainsaw, motorcycle, or other motorized equipment that is stored away for part of the year.

• **Lead substitutes.** Cars built before the introduction of catalytic converters used leaded fuel, which boosted octane and helped lubricate the valves. These additives are designed to help replace the power and lubrication lost in today's unleaded gas.

OIL ADDITIVES

These all have the same goal: to help reduce friction between the engine's moving parts, which provides several advantages:

• Greater power and acceleration

• Less engine wear, longer engine life

• Quieter operation

• Easier starts

• **Oil boosters** are designed to improve oil's "thickness" (make it more slippery) to improve its performance: Better lubrication helps at cold starts. For engines that burn oil, these additives are designed to help make it harder for the oil to get past the piston rings.

• **Friction reducers** provide additional lubrication beyond what traditional oil can. Some use specialized chemicals for this purpose, like PFTE (Teflon®).

• **Metal treatments** work on the engine itself rather than the oil. They help reduce friction by creating a smoother surface on the metal.

- **Smoke treatments** reduce exhaust smoke and oil burning by thickening the engine oil. They also help give added protection to valve seals, piston rings, and cylinder walls.

- **Engine oil flush.** Even if you change your oil regularly, harmful deposits can form in your crankcase and oiling system. You use these products when you change the oil, which helps remove sludge, gums, varnish, and combustion deposits.

OTHER ADDITIVES

There is a wide selection of fluids to help keep your car in good working order, as well as ones that help solve minor problems and prevent major service headaches.

- **Stop leak additives** . . . er, stop minor leaks. There are additives for coolant, engine oil, transmission fluid, power steering fluid, and air-conditioning systems. They work by expanding and conditioning seals and gaskets that have dried out or shrunk.

- **Transmission treatments and conditioners** help provide additional lubrication to provide smoother shifting and longer transmission life.

- **Coolant service products** include radiator flush, cleaner lubricants, and antirust products, all to help maintain your radiator's cooling capacity. These are especially useful for older cars, high-performance engines, and cars that tend to run hot or overheat.

Detailing

You can give your car a good wash and wax from time to time, but if you want to clean and *protect* the complete car, you're talking about *detailing.*

Detailing includes a comprehensive cleaning of the interior and exterior of the car, as well as taking steps to help preserve and protect the appearance of your car's paint, plastic, upholstery, rugs, wheels, and tires. Not only does keeping up your car's appearance make your rides more enjoyable, it helps protect your investment. You can kiss the Blue Book value good-bye with too many scratches and a funky smell in the passenger seat.

SUPPLIES

- Car wash liquid (pH balanced is preferred)
- Tar and bug remover
- All-purpose cleaner
- Carpet shampoo or cleaner
- Tire and trim dressing
- Upholstery and/or leather cleaners
- Interior dressing (silicone protectant)
- Window cleaner
- Wax/cleaner/sealer
- Clay cleaner

EQUIPMENT

- Soft cotton washing mitt
- Clean rags or towels (very clean. One spot of grit and it's all over.)
- Paper towels to clean the windows
- Soft bristle brush
- Wheel cleaning brush
- Detail brushes
- Plastic bucket
- Sheepskin chamois, synthetic chamois, or drying towels

- Car sponges or terry towels

- Hose and water

- Wet/dry vacuum

- Rug steam cleaner (optional)

- Orbital buffer (optional)

- Q-Tips or detailing brushes

The Exterior

WASHING AND WAXING YOUR CAR

Never do it in direct sunlight. Find a good, shady spot and make sure the car's surface is cool. Start by thoroughly rinsing your car off from the top down (not *with* the top down), removing all surface dirt, mud, or grime to prevent scratches when you're washing the finish.

Remove Bugs and Road Tar

Using the tar and bug remover on a sponge or rag, remove any bugs or road tar. Rinse.

Clean Doorjambs and Moldings

Use an all-purpose cleaner and sponge to clean them and the hatch/trunk areas. Don't use normal car wash here—it's hard to rinse the soap from these areas without getting the interior too wet. Scrub body side moldings with a soft brush and the same all-purpose cleaner—but don't scrub the car's paint! Rinse it all off with water.

Wash the Car by Hand

Caution: Never use dish detergent or a scrub brush on your car's painted surfaces. The dish soap can damage and dry out your finish, and some brushes can actually create hairline scratches that will eventually compromise your car's finish. Use a gentle car wash and sponges, terry cloths, or a detailing mitt.

Start from the top and work your way down, in small sections that you rinse when you're done. Never soap up the entire car—this may leave a film on your finish. Rinse repeatedly from the top down to make sure all the soap is removed. Make sure you thoroughly clean any areas you treated with the bug and tar remover.

Stubborn Stains and Dirt

For hard-to-remove spots, there are automotive finish clay cleaners and other specialty products that can help remove dirt that can't be washed off with car wash soap. Clay is the best "Pre-wax" as it makes waxing your car easier.

Drying the Car

As temptingly easy as it may seem, *never let your car air dry*—especially if you're using hard water. It can leave streaks and create water marks that may damage your paint. Use a synthetic or sheepskin chamois to remove most of the water. As you complete each section, rinse it in clean water and wring it out thoroughly. Finish drying the car with a soft cotton towel.

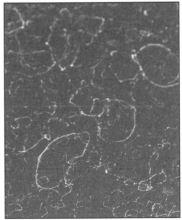

Cleaning the Wheels

Begin by scrubbing them with the wheel brush and car wash solution. Rinse repeatedly as you work. You may need a small brush to get into the areas where hot brake dust bonds to the wheels.

Special wheel cleaners are available and are recommended, but read the precautions on the label before using. Check your owner's manual to see if your rims have a "clear coat"; if they do, only use wheel cleaners specifically marked as safe for them.

Thoroughly rinse wheels with water.

Tire and Trim Dressing

Tires and other synthetic rubber parts of your car's exterior will dry out and turn gray over time. A variety of products are available to help these parts retain their black color and prevent damage from the sun's ultraviolet rays. Apply the appropriate treatments to the tires, black rubber trim, and moldings. Most dressings are sold as sprays, but be careful not to get them on painted surfaces or your driveway (they will stain the concrete). If necessary, apply some to a rag first, then to the rubber.

Waxing Prolific About Waxing

Sit-com perfect images of suburban dads washing and waxing their shiny cars make it look like the easiest thing in the world, but the whole process can actually be a little more complicated than you might have guessed. Read carefully.

Preparing Your Car for Waxing

Always wash before you wax. Waxing a dirty car can damage the paint.

CHOOSING YOUR WAX

There are a wide variety of products available to "wax" your car. Some traditional products may actually contain natural wax, but many modern products are actually formulated from synthetic compounds. The basic idea behind waxing is to provide a barrier that adds gloss to the finish and protects the car's paint from the elements. Whether natural or synthetic, all of them eventually wear away and must be reapplied. Some waxes are simple protective barriers that add gloss to the finish. Others combine cleaners and sealants with wax. Still others are multistep applications with separate products for cleaning, sealing, and waxing.

The wax that's best may depend on how new your car is and how often it has already been waxed. For newer and frequently waxed cars, a simple one-step wax can do the job. For a car that hasn't been waxed recently, products that include cleaners and sealants might be better.

NOTE: If you do wax often, make sure you're using a product with very low or nonabrasive ingredients.

WAXING YOUR CAR

- Read and follow the instructions on your wax carefully.

- Use a clean, soft, lint-free cloth or micro fiber cloth to remove the dried wax.

- Change cloths (not clothes) often to avoid leaving wax residue on the paint.

- Always work on a small section at a time. Don't move to the next section until you've finished buffing the dried wax off the first section.

- Take your time and avoid getting wax in cracks and rubber trim.

- Double-check each panel to make sure all the wax has been wiped down.

- If the wax has left a dusty film on the car, rinse it down with water and then dry it with a chamois. (Sheepskin or synthetic)

- Finally, buff the finish with a fresh, clean cloth.

Caution on Using a Buffer

Used properly, a buffer can save you a lot of time and energy. Follow the manufacturer's instructions carefully and use a soft, clean buffing pad. Keep it moving—you can damage the finish if you stay in one spot too long. Use only an orbital buffer intended for use with auto finishes. Other kinds can leave permanent swirl marks or even remove the paint from your car!

Another Caution: Clear Coat Finishes

Most of today's cars have a clear coat applied at the factory. It's sprayed on over the base coat to create a high-gloss finish. Clear coat is paint, not a paint treatment, so treat it like paint. Wash and wax frequently to protect it from the elements. Some older products can damage these finishes, so use only clear-coat-safe cleaners and waxes to maintain it properly.

The Final Details

Remove any excess wax from the cracks and emblems with a detail brush and a towel. Don't forget to wax air dams, rocker panels, door-jambs, and rear hatch areas!

THE INTERIOR

Thought you were done, huh?

Vacuum All Areas Thoroughly

Remove the floor mats and make sure you get into tight spots and compartments where dirt can build up, such as between the seats and in the console. If the headliner, sun visors, and door panels are fabric, vacuum these as well.

Shampooing the Interior

There are three approaches to shampooing:

- **Spray-on shampoos** are easy to apply and dry quickly. Your car can be ready to go as soon as you vacuum up the dried shampoo residue. The foam itself does the cleaning, so keep the use of additional water to a minimum to help your interior dry faster.

- **Carpet steam cleaners** take considerably longer than spray-on shampoo and the carpets remain damp for a longer time. However, steam cleaners can provide a much more thorough cleaning and allow you to treat hard-to-clean spots repeatedly.

- **Liquid shampoos** provide some of the cleaning power of a steam cleaner but require even more effort and take even longer to dry.

You may need to pretreat heavy stains in the carpet and fabrics. Use a stiff brush to scrape off dried food and other debris before you shampoo. Whichever method you use, follow the directions carefully and use the same procedure for carpets in the trunk or hatchback areas as well.

Cleaning the Upholstery

You can use either spray-on cleaners or a steam cleaner; just don't scrub the upholstery as hard as you would the carpets—you could damage the fabric.

Leather Seats

If you're lucky enough to have them, clean the seats or door panels with saddle soap or an appropriate leather cleaner and conditioner. Don't use mink oil, fabric stain remover, or rubber or vinyl protectants on leather interiors—they will damage your nice, expensive seats.

Headliner and Sun Visors

Fabric ones can be cleaned with upholstery cleaner or shampoo. For heavy stains use a fabric stain remover. If your headliner and sun visors are vinyl, clean them with a window or all-purpose cleaner.

Floor Mats

Vacuum carpeted floor mats thoroughly and shampoo them as you did the interior carpets. Rubber ones can be cleaned with an all-purpose cleaner. Make sure both the mats and the carpet are completely dry before putting them back in to avoid new and permanent traveling companions (e.g., mold and mildew).

Dashboard and Interior Vinyl Surfaces

Clean the dashboard and interior vinyl with a rag dampened with diluted all-purpose cleaner. Keep moisture to a minimum and avoid get-

ting water into the electronics on the dashboard and in the door panels. Follow up with a fresh rag dampened with plain water and dry all the surfaces with towels to avoid streaking. Hard-to-reach spots such as air vent louvers can be cleaned with Q-Tips or a small paintbrush.

Interior Dressings

These are designed to protect the interior surface from the drying and cracking caused by age, ultraviolet light, and extreme temperatures.

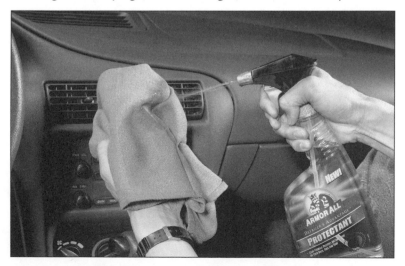

Many use silicone to help keep plastic surfaces looking new. To avoid overspray stains, apply the product to a rag and then wipe on.

Treat all interior plastic and vinyl surfaces except the steering wheel (it would make it slippery). Do not use silicone on leather. Nongloss dressings are available to minimize dashboard glare and reflection in the windshield.

And Speaking of Windshields: Cleaning the Windows

Do not spray glass cleaner on them directly. Use the rag method mentioned above to avoid overspray. Wipe windows down thoroughly with the glass cleaner and dry with a soft rag or paper towel.

Engine Detailing

Years ago a complete detailing would include steam cleaning the engine compartment. Today's engines and engine compartments are tightly packed with sophisticated and sensitive electronics that can be easily damaged. Steam cleaning is not advised. There are a variety of spray-on engine cleaners and degreasers available, but these must be used carefully. Use a spray-on foaming degreaser and wash off with low-pressure water. If you're not sure what's safe, leave it to the professionals.

The Garage and Workshop

It's important for any driver to maintain an organized, well-stocked garage or workshop. Be sure to have everything you need at hand, including lift equipment (jacks and jack stands or ramps), battery chargers, an air compressor and air tools for avid do-it-yourselfers, power tools with accessories, hand tools, and a place to store all of this stuff. Organization is just as important as the tools themselves. Outfit your garage or workshop with tables, cabinets, and shelving systems. Get a comfortable stool to sit on when working or a creeper to make getting under your properly lifted vehicle easy for you. You'll find just about everything you need for your garage or workshop at your local Pep Boys store.

CHAPTER 6

A Timeline of Cars, America, and the Pep Boys

"Manny, Moe, and Jack are the three best symbols a firm ever had. The mere mention of their names is enough to raise a chuckle."

—Philadelphia Inquirer (March 3, 1986)

FROM The Pep Boys—Manny, Moe and Jack:
Founders of the Automotive Aftermarket
by Marian Calabro

1857   Liquid gasoline is developed.

1860   The first internal combustion engine is patented in Paris, France.

1887   Ransom Olds, later known for the Oldsmobile, builds the first steam-propelled car in the United States.

1891   William Morrison builds the first electric car in the United States.

1896   The Duryea brothers build the first gas-powered car in the United States.

Henry Ford, working on his own, builds his first car.

Emmanuel "Manny" Rosenfeld is born on February 6 in Philadelphia.

1897   Maurice "Moe" Strauss is born on March 20 in Philadelphia.

1900   The first U.S. car show takes place at New York's Madison Square Garden. Thirty manufacturers have vehicles on display.

1903   Henry Ford starts The Ford Motor Company.

1904   Ford introduces the two-cylinder Model A.

1905   Racing at Daytona Beach, Florida, becomes a popular annual event.

1908   Ford introduces the 20-horsepower Model T, the first afford-able car. More than 15 million Model Ts, nicknamed "Tin Lizzies," will be manufactured through 1927.

William Durant, an executive at Ford, leaves to form his own company, General Motors. He does it by buying up Buick, Cadillac, and other small manufacturers.

1910   GM's Cadillac division produces the first U.S. car with an elec-tric self-starter.

1913   Ford installs assembly lines. As production efficiency in-creases, the price of a Model T drops from $850 to $440 to $275.

1916   The U.S. Congress passes the first Federal Road Act, but few roads are built due to America's entry into World War I the fol-lowing year.

1921   Manny Rosenfeld, Moe Strauss, and W. Graham "Jack" Jack-son open Pep Auto Supply Company at 7-11 North 63rd Street, Philadelphia. Moe Radavitz is also a partner.

Passage of the first Federal Highway Act launches the idea of an interstate road system. The Bureau of Public Roads creates a system of highway numbering: even numbers for east-west roads, odd numbers for north-south.

1923   Manny Rosenfeld and Moe Strauss drive a Model T to south-ern California to investigate the marketplace. A dress shop called Minnie, Maude & Mabel's catches their eye. On return-ing to Philadelphia, they change their company's name to The Pep Boys—Manny, Moe & Jack.

Moe Radavitz and Jack Jackson leave the business. The face of Moe Strauss's brother Isadore, who works for Pep Boys from 1923 to 1928, replaces Jack's face in the logo.

1925   The Pep Boys—Manny, Moe & Jack incorporates in Pennsylvania.

Walter P. Chrysler, who ran the Buick division of General Motors, leaves to open his own company, The Chrysler Corporation.

In the beginning, Pep Boys storefronts were typically narrow with deep backroom storage areas, much different from the retail and service Supercenters of today.

1926   The Bureau of Public Roads maps Route 66, planned to stretch from Lake Michigan to the Pacific Ocean in southern California.

1927   Ford discontinues the Model T and introduces a fancier four-cylinder car, advertised as "a roadster for Youth and the Country Club." It is given the same name as Ford's 1908 two-cylinder offering: Model A.

Pep Boys establishes the first unconditional one-year guarantee on tires, without raising prices. Competitors soon follow suit.

1928   Manny's brother Murray Rosenfeld joins the company.

1929   General Motors introduces America's first six-cylinder car, the Chevrolet "Stovebolt."

Detroit produces over five million cars.

The stock market crashes, ushering in the Great Depression. New car sales fall by 75 percent through 1932.

1931   Pep Boys issues almost 700,000 copies of a 100-page, two-color merchandise catalog. Sales grow as Americans need to keep their old cars running.

Pep Boys sells 6 million gallons of gasoline annually.

1932–33 Pep Boys creates a separate corporation called The Pep Boys— Manny, Moe & Jack of California. Under the leadership of Murray Rosenfeld, the first two stores open in Los Angeles in 1933.

On February 14, 1933, Pep Boys opened its first two stores in Los Angeles, California. With the demand for automotive parts and accessories increasing with West Coast population growth, Angelenos have made Pep Boys part of their car culture.

1934   Unlike most employers during the Depression, Pep Boys does not cut salaries. In fact, vigorous growth allows Pep Boys of California to raise salaries by 18 percent.

1936–37 The auto manufacturing industry unionizes.

1940   Thanks to the Works Progress Administration and other programs under President Franklin D. Roosevelt's New Deal, the United States finally has a paved system of roads from coast to coast.

1941   The United States enters World War II.

1942   Pep Boys begins and fully funds a Pension Trust Plan for long-term employees.

Car assembly lines shut down as the use of steel is forbidden for nondefense products. Chrysler produces Sherman tanks. Ford produces B-24 Liberator bombers.

Pep Boys stores in the 1940s were noted for their window displays featuring Manny, Moe, and Jack as well as the large, Art Deco–styled sign titled "The Pep Boys Auto Supplies," common to Pep Boys stores of the era.

Rubber is scarce, leading to a surge of sales in tire patch kits.

1945   World War II ends. Half of all cars in the United States are at least ten years old. Rather than spend time designing new models, car makers manufacture their old models in order to meet huge postwar consumer demand.

1946   Pep Boys becomes a public company listed on the American Stock Exchange. (The California Pep Boys, a separate corporation, is not part of the offering.)

1947   Pep Boys moves its general offices in Philadelphia from Fifth and Courtland Streets to 3111 West Allegheny Avenue, which originally contained a warehouse and offices. (The building is no longer a warehouse but remains the company's headquarters.)

Pep Boys sells merchandise on credit for the first time since the Great Depression.

Studebaker introduces the first car designed after the war.

California authorizes the building of a new type of fast road called the freeway.

1948   The "Big Three" automakers (Ford, Chrysler, and General Motors) all introduce new models. GM's Cadillac, with its tail fins, sets a trend for car design throughout the 1950s.

1950   Pep Boys reaches its post–World War II goal of sixty stores. Further expansion is put on hold due to shortages of automotive supplies.

The company begins an unbroken chain of paying cash dividends to shareholders.

1953   Pep Boys experiments with television by sponsoring baseball games from Griffith Stadium in Washington, D.C.

The Chevrolet Corvette power-top convertible becomes one of America's most sought-after cars.

1954   Ford joins the sports car trend with the first Thunderbird.

1955   The company establishes The Pep Boys Educational Foundation, which provides college scholarships to children of employees.

1956   Carmakers offer air-conditioning as an option for the first time.

   The Interstate Highway Act funds a nationwide system of toll-free roads. Some 41,000 miles of roads will be built through 1966, at a cost of $54 billion.

1957   The United States faces a financial recession and a blow to its pride when Russia launches the spacecraft Sputnik. Funds are diverted to the Cold War. Smaller, more gas-efficient cars such as the American Motors Rambler are introduced.

1958   Pep Boys partners with Diners Club to offer a customer charge program.

   The company enlarges the warehouse portion of its Allegheny Avenue building by 10,000 square feet in order to warehouse its own tires. The expansion costs $109,000.

   The first Volkswagen Beetle is sold in the United States.

1959   Cofounder Emmanuel "Manny" Rosenfeld dies. His son Lester, who joined the company in 1946, is named to the board of directors.

   Pep Boys pays off its mortgage on 3111 West Allegheny Avenue, now owning its headquarters building free and clear.

1961   Two companies officially become one as the Philadelphia-based The Pep Boys—Manny, Moe & Jack acquires The Pep Boys—Manny, Moe & Jack of California.

   The company expands into Texas under the leadership of Robert P. Strauss, Moe's son.

   The United States establishes a military presence in Vietnam.

1964   Pep Boys' Texas subsidiary is merged into the parent corporation.

   The economical but fun-to-drive Ford Mustang is an instant success. Competitors counter with such "muscle cars" as the Chevrolet Camaro and the Plymouth Barracuda.

1966   In the wake of Ralph Nader's 1965 book *Unsafe at Any Speed* (an indictment of the Chevrolet Corvair), cars begin to have seat belts.

As this 1960s-era storefront proves, Pep Boys specialized in eye-catching window displays
that could pique anyone's curiosity. Showing everything from swing sets to bicycles
and tires, customers were always sure to see something in the window they needed
for their home or vehicle.

1969   Sales of foreign cars top 1 million in the U.S. However, large
        and midsized cars still account for 72 percent of all U.S. sales.

1970   The Clean Air Act gives automakers six years to cut emissions
        in new cars by 90 percent.

1971   Pep Boys begins to close smaller, outmoded stores and dis-
        bands its Texas operation.

1973   Benjamin Strauss, Moe's son, is named president. Moe re-
        mains company chairman.

        U.S. troops leave Vietnam after a ceasefire is declared.

        The Arab oil embargo forces Americans to line up for gas, and
        ushers in 55-mile-per-hour speed limits nationally.

        The economic climate worsens as inflation and interest rates
        rise. Pep Boys fights back with new and improved stores and
        more aggressive promotions.

A circa 1970s store uniform patch prominently displays Manny, Moe, and Jack.

1975   Pep Boys' sales top $100 million for the first time. The company rebuilds a California warehouse damaged by fire the year before and capitalizes on two national crazes by selling citizens band radios and recreational vehicle accessories.

1976   Pep Boys begins an ambitious program of store remodeling, aimed at making stores more self-service oriented. This allows outlets to carry up to 8,000 items, more than any offered by competitors.

Sunday openings become the norm for most Pep Boys stores in the East.

The company shifts from a six-day to a five-day work week at its stores "without a corresponding reduction in individual compensation."

1978   Moe steps down as chairman, but stays on as a company director and chairman emeritus.

Pep Boys announces that its emphasis will be on large, free-standing stores with extensive service capabilities.

The company introduces AutoSense, one of the industry's first diagnostic computer systems. It also begins computerizing its sales and inventory functions.

1979   Pep Boys opens its largest store to date, a 26,000-square-foot Garden Grove facility in Anaheim, California.

Auto sound equipment becomes a growth center for Pep Boys.

Mitchell Leibovitz joins the company as vice president of finance.

Murray Rosenfeld dies.

1980   In its most aggressive expansion in a decade, Pep Boys opens
        nine new stores.

        The company becomes a television sponsor of the Philadel-
        phia Phillies, airing commercials with Manny, Moe, and Jack
        as animated characters.

        In prudent response to interest rates nearing 20 percent, the
        company prepays all variable rate mortgages and replaces its
        in-house credit sales with an outside credit card program.

        Japan overtakes the United States as the world's largest car
        manufacturer.

        Near insolvency, Chrysler secures a loan guarantee of $1.2 bil-
        lion from the U.S. government.

1981   Pep Boys expands its TV sponsorships to the Philadelphia Ea-
        gles and Los Angeles Rams.

1982   Cofounder Maurice "Moe" Strauss dies in Beverly Hills,
        California.

        Morton A. "Bud" Krause becomes president and chief operat-
        ing officer. Benjamin Strauss continues as chairman and adds
        the CEO title.

        Pep Boys stock moves to the New York Stock Exchange (ticker
        symbol PBY).

        The company opens eleven new stores and begins building
        two new warehouses. A milestone is the Los Angeles flagship
        on Washington Boulevard, a 40,000-square-foot facility with
        twenty-three service bays.

        Japanese carmaker Honda opens a plant in Ohio, sending
        shock waves through Detroit.

1984   Unique in the field, Pep Boys commits itself to the "automo-
        tive superstore" concept and national expansion. Service and
        repair are the fastest-growing business segments.

        Chrysler achieves financial turnaround with sales of $2.4
        billion.

1986   Mitchell G. Leibovitz becomes the first non–founding family member to be president of Pep Boys. Benjamin Strauss remains chairman and CEO.

An expanded point-of-sale program enhances the company's purchasing, distribution, and financial systems.

Many competitors merge or are acquired. Pep Boys remains independent, introducing an ambitious $475 million "Five-Year Plan" to expand its distribution, upgrade its systems, and double its store count.

1987   Pep Boys introduces TV ads with Manny, Moe, and Jack as three-dimensional animated figures.

1988   Pep Boys consolidates headquarters and administrative functions to Philadelphia to centralize its organizational structure for better efficiency.

Company stores stop selling bicycles and begin selling name-brand tires.

1990   Pep Boys introduces the Banner Service program for excellence in customer service.

1991   Pep Boys sales top $1 billion for the first time.

Steady monthly sales increases follow the company's conversion from Sale Price/Regular Price to Everyday Low Prices.

The company completes its conversion to branded parts.

The first "warehouse unit store," in Exton, Pennsylvania, opens. The company modifies existing stores on this new model, which offers a more user-friendly shopping environment.

General Motors starts the Saturn division.

1992   Benjamin Strauss retires as chairman, but remains on the board of directors.

Four Pep Boys stores are destroyed during civil unrest in Los Angeles following the infamous Rodney King trial. Local citizens defend the store on Hollywood Boulevard.

All stores convert to the PIR (perpetual inventory/automatic replenishment) system.

The company focuses on a three-tiered customer base: do-it-yourself, do-it-for-me, and the professional technician. It is the only aftermarket retailer capable of serving all three groups.

Pep Boys publishes its first bilingual catalogs for selected Hispanic markets.

Service managers, along with district and regional field management teams, are required to be certified by the Institute for Automotive Service Excellence (ASE).

1993   All Pep Boys stores are open seven days and six nights a week (where legally permitted).

All service centers implement an electronic work order program.

The company repositions its tire line and creates the position of tire specialist.

Pep Boys registers its website www.pepboys.com.

1994   Mitchell G. Leibovitz is elected chairman.

The company opens its first "Concept 4 Supercenter" in Broomall, Pennsylvania. An additional fifty stores are converted to warehouse-format Supercenters.

The company begins to establish maintenance relationships with national auto fleets.

1995   Pep Boys celebrates its entry into Puerto Rico and the opening of its five-hundredth store.

1996   Pep Boys underwrites *Road Ready*, a car repair program on The Nashville Network, a cable television channel.

1998   Pep Boys solidifies its position as the industry leader in service and tire sales.

1999   Pep Boys expands truck and SUV sections in almost 500 stores.

The company consolidates its distribution function into a 400,000-square-foot warehouse in Chester, New York.

For the first time in company history, do-it-for-me customers (rather than do-it-yourselfers) account for a majority of store revenues.

2000   Pep Boys adds a vehicle evaluation program to tap into the $361 billion used-car marketplace.

The company introduces a $70 million Profit Enhancement Plan (PEP).

2001   The PEP initiative results in savings of $84 million.

Company stock achieves the seventh highest percentage increase on the New York Stock Exchange.

2002   George Babich, chief financial officer, adds the role of president. Mitchell G. Leibovitz remains chairman and CEO.

Online shopping for 120,000 accessories and tires is introduced at www.pepboys.com.

Rebranded "Pep Express Parts," the company's auto parts delivery business operates from 450 stores and 1,300 delivery trucks.

2003   Mitchell G. Leibovitz retires as chairman and CEO.

Bernard Korman becomes chairman.

Lawrence N. Stevenson joins the company as CEO and a member of the board of directors.

Corporate restructuring results in the closing of 33 of the company's 629 stores (approximately 5 percent) and a subsequent reduction of about 3 percent of store employees.

Stores introduce new product categories such as personal transportation items, including electric and gas scooters, resulting in higher year-to-year sales by the third quarter.

2004   Store remodeling begins.

New product categories are added, including Personal Transportation, Travel, and Garage.

New logo and brand identity are unveiled.

Branded tires rejoin the Pep Boys lineup.

Customer Satisfaction Index (CSI) is initiated.

Express Service is introduced, focusing on core repairs and maintenance services.

A new Pep Boys Auto Supercenter.

CHAPTER 7

Glossary of Terms

Air filter Keeps dirt and particles from entering the engine with the air needed for combustion.

Alignment The position of the wheels and suspension; alignment problems cause the car to pull to one side or drive erratically.

Alternator Charges the **battery** with "new" electricity; powered by the engine.

Balance A wheel is out of balance when its weight is uneven in different places; corrected by service technicians with metal weights.

Battery Stores electricity so you can start your car and provides electricity to all the components that need it.

Brake calipers On disc brakes, these "grab" the rotor with the brake pads to make the wheel stop.

Brake fluid Forced from the **master cylinder** into the brakes (both drum and disc), forcing **pistons** out against the **calipers** or **shoes,** causing the wheel to stop.

Brake lining On drum brakes, the surface (on the inside of the drum) whose friction against the **brake shoes** causes the wheel to stop.

Brake pad On disc brakes, the surface that the **calipers** grab and force against the **rotor,** causing the wheel to stop.

Brake shoes In drum brakes, the parts that push out against the **brake lining,** causing the wheel to stop.

Catalytic converter Converts more toxic waste fumes into less harmful water and carbon dioxide. Regular inspections and service on this keeps your car from failing an emissions test.

Clutch Moves the engine onto the transmission or gear box—in manual cars, the driver manually releases it to change gears.

Coil (or ignition coil) Turns a tiny amount of electricity into serious voltage to the spark plugs so it can ignite the gas/air mixture.

Control arms A pair of rods that go from the body of the car to the wheels, connecting them together with the shocks or suspension system cradled in the middle.

Coolant Fluid, usually in a 50/50 mix with water that circulates around the engine to keep it cool.

Crankshaft The "pedals" of the engine that pistons push down on and cause to rotate, driving your car.

Current The amount of flow of electricity.

Cylinder The housing inside which the gas and air explosion occurs, pushing the piston down against the **crankshaft.**

Differential Turns the **crankshaft's** spin 90 degrees to drive the wheels (think of the crossed top of a T), and determines the *difference* in wheel speed when the car makes a turn.

Exhaust manifold A bunch of pipes near the engine where the car breathes out, the first step on the way to the tailpipe.

Fuel filter C'mon. Self-explanatory, right?

Fuel pump Pushes the gas from the tank into the engine.

(Hydraulic) master cylinder Pushes out brake fluid when you step on the brake pedal, which then travels down brake lines and up into the brakes (see **brake fluid, brake pad,** and **brake shoes**).

Intake valve Closes and opens, allowing gas and air to enter the cylinder to be ignited by the spark.

Knock/Ping Noise created when there is a misfire in the combustion chamber; often occurs when too low an octane is being burned.

Muffler Quiets the explosions and noise of the engine.

Octane The number that determines the likelihood of gas knocking or pinging.

PCV valve Catches gaseous fuel that has escaped into the rest of the engine and sends it back in to be combusted properly.

Piston In the "engine as bicyclist" metaphor, the "foot" that is pushed down by combustion against the "pedal" of the **crankshaft,** causing it to turn.

Radiator Doesn't *heat* the car—helps heat escape from the engine, keeping it cool!

Radiator cap The cooling system needs to be pressurized properly to work; besides just being a normal fill cap, a radiator cap helps keep that pressure.

Reservoir Where excess coolant is stored; it keeps the overflow when heat makes the fluid expand.

Rotor (brake disc) Turns with the wheel of a car. On disc brakes, **brake fluid** pushes against **pistons,** which cause **calipers** to close and grab the disc against the **brake lining,** causing the rotor, and therefore the wheel, to stop.

Shock absorber/strut Like the mechanism that slows the swinging of a storm door, this absorbs much of the "bounce" when the car goes over a bump.

Solenoid An electronic switch—usually used to refer to the one that allows electricity to flow to the engine when you insert and turn your key.

Spark plug Creates the spark that ignites the fuel and air, which causes the combustion that pushes the piston down against the **crankshaft** and makes your car go!

Spring Keeps the tire on the ground by compressing and expanding, pushing the wheel down and pulling it up, depending on the road's surface.

Starter motor An electric motor that starts the engine by spinning the **crankshaft** mechanically (before combustion begins to occur).

Transaxle In front-wheel drive, the **transmission** and **differential** all in one.

Transmission The gears that sit in between the engine and the wheels, determining the car's power.

Universal joint/CV joint An "elbow" in the driveshaft that allows the car some flexibility as it hits bumps or changes direction without snapping the whole drivetrain in half.

Wheel cylinders On drum brakes, they press the **brake shoes** out against the **brake lining** to stop the wheels.

CHAPTER 8

Important Records for You to Keep

CAR SPECIFICATIONS

Here's a place you can write down everything you might need quickly, whether you're changing your oil or speaking to a technician. While most of it can be found in your owner's manual, things such as the tire pressure might be on the inside doorjamb on the driver's side, and engine size on the underside of the hood.

Make	
Model	
Year	
License plate #	
VIN #	
Insurance company	
Policy #	
Insurance company phone number	
Number of cylinders	
Engine size (usually in liters)	
Octane of gas required	
Gas tank capacity	
Type of oil needed	
Type of coolant & percentage-to-water ratio	
PSI for front tires	
PSI for rear tires	
MPG city/highway	

SERVICE RECORD

Believe us—keeping track of what you had done and when will not only help you keep your car running smoothly, it will also save you headaches and bucks. On the "big" services, always check the invoice to see if the technician did everything your maintenance schedule demands.

Date	Mileage	Service(s) Performed	Cost

Date	Mileage	Service(s) Performed	Cost

INDEX

ABOUT THE AUTHOR

E. J. Braswell comes from a long line of gearheads on both sides of the family—Botnick *and* Braswell. If E. J. were a car, it would be a '57 Chevy pickup.

Pep Boys Coupon Offers

FREE Summer Travel Maintenance Special

Free Air-Conditioning Performance Check includes Summer Travel Courtesy Inspection. Entire service checks air-conditioning, belts, hoses, tires, and fluids!

Retail Promotion (E)

Limit one per household. Cannot be combined with other offers or coupons.

Coupon Good 5/1/2005 - 9/1/2005

One FREE Oil Change Upgrade

Upgrade your oil. Buy a standard ProLine, name brand, or semi-synthetic oil change and upgrade to a name brand, semi-synthetic or synthetic oil for the same price as your entry-level oil change with this coupon!

Retail Promotion (E)

Limit one per household. Cannot be combined with other offers or coupons.

Coupon Good 5/1/2005 - 12/31/2005

FREE Winter Weather Maintenance Check

Free Starting & Charging System Analysis includes Winter Weather Courtesy Inspection. Entire service checks battery, starter, belts, hoses, tires, and fluids!

Retail Promotion (E)

Limit one per household. Cannot be combined with other offers or coupons.

Coupon Good 9/1/2005 - 12/1/2005

PEPBOYS AUTO

To find a store near you call 1-800-PEP BOYS or visit www.pepboys.com